The Violence of

The Violence of Love

Oscar Romero

Compiled and translated by
James R. Brockman, S. J.

ORBIS BOOKS
Maryknoll, New York 10545

Founded in 1970, Orbis Books endeavors to publish works that enlighten the mind, nourish the spirit, and challenge the conscience. The publishing arm of the Maryknoll Fathers and Brothers, Orbis seeks to explore the global dimensions of the Christian faith and mission, to invite dialogue with diverse cultures and religious traditions, and to serve the cause of reconciliation and peace. The books published reflect the views of their authors and do not represent the official position of the Maryknoll Society. To learn more about Maryknoll and Orbis Books, please visit our website at www.maryknoll.org.

Originally published in 1988 by Harper & Row, Publishers, San Francisco and in Canada by Fitzhenry & Whiteside, Limited, Toronto.

This edition published in 2004 by Orbis Books, Maryknoll, NY 10545, by arrangement with the Plough Publishing House.

Cover woodcut by Robert McGovern.

Manufactured in the United States of America.

ORBIS/ISBN 1-57075-535-3

The Library of Congress has catalogued the original edition as follows:

Romero, Oscar A. (Oscar Arnulfo), 1917–1980
     The violence of love : the wisdom of Oscar Romero / Oscar Romero ; compiled and translated by James R. Brockman ; foreword by Henri J.M. Nouwen.
          p. cm.
     Originally published: San Francisco : Harper & Row, c1988.
     ISBN 0-87486-951-X (softcover)
     1. Meditations. I. Brockman, James R. II. Title.
[BX2186.R594 1998]
     252'. 02—dc21   97-51460
                                                           CIP

THE VIOLENCE we preach is not
the violence of the sword,
the violence of hatred.
It is the violence of love,
of brotherhood,
the violence that wills to beat weapons
into sickles for work.

OSCAR ROMERO, NOVEMBER 27, 1977

Contents

Foreword   ix
Preface   xv
Translator's Note   xvii

CHAPTER ONE
A Pilgrim Church   1

CHAPTER TWO
A History of Salvation   21

CHAPTER THREE
The Idol of Self   39

CHAPTER FOUR
Don't Pull Them Up   67

CHAPTER FIVE
Evangelizer of the People   95

CHAPTER SIX
God's Justice   119

CHAPTER SEVEN
The Bright Light of Christ   137

CHAPTER EIGHT
Option for the Poor   161

CHAPTER NINE
Good News to the Poor   185

Notes   207
Other Titles from Plough   215

Foreword

I JUST FINISHED READING the collection of quotations from
Archbishop Romero that James Brockman has so ably brought
together in this book. As I was reading I felt as if his spirit was
drawing me closer and closer to the truth, that is, the true relationship with God. When I finally reached his last words, a
deep silence came over me, and I realized that something new
had happened to me.

It is not easy to give words to this spiritual event that took
place during the reading of Oscar Romero's unpretentious, un-
adorned, and unambiguous words. Maybe the best way to sum-
marize what happened to me is to say that I had encountered a
man of God marked by humility and confidence, calling me to
conversion and action. In this foreword I want to express more
fully the meaning of this encounter. Thus I hope to offer a spiritual place in which a similar encounter can take place for the
many who will read this book.

Oscar Romero is a humble man of God. His humility per-
vades all he says. That probably is the main reason why it was
possible for me to read these very challenging and demanding
words. They are spoken by someone who is very close to me.
Oscar Romero does not speak from a distance. He does not
hide his fears, his brokenness, his hesitations. There is a warmth
in his words that opens my heart to listen. It is as if he puts his
arm around my shoulder and slowly walks with me. He shares
with me my struggles: "God knows how hard it was for me [to
become archbishop]. How timid I have felt before you..." He
explains to me who he wants to be for his people: "The attitude
to be taken...is not 'I'm in charge here!'...You are only a human
being...You must...serve the people according to God's will
and not according to your whim." He does not want to be

different: "The shepherd does not want security while they give no security to his flock." He is aware that he receives as much as he gives: "Precisely in those charisms that the Spirit gives to the people the bishop finds the touchstone of his authenticity." "With this people it is not hard to be a good shepherd. They are a people that impel to their service..." He asks for forgiveness and prayer: "I beg pardon for not having shown all the fortitude the gospel asks..." "I ask your prayers to be faithful – that I will not abandon my people but that together with them I will run all the risks that my ministry demands." As I hear him speak to me in this way, I know that he is indeed the good shepherd who lays down his life for his friends. He lays down for me his own broken humanity, his fears, his sins, his hopes, and thus opens my heart to listen to his words of faith.

Oscar Romero's humility is the fruitful ground of his confidence. He is a man *con fide*, with trust, an unlimited trust in Jesus Christ. As I listen to him I realize that I am listening to a man who has fixed his eyes on Jesus and thus can walk safely amidst the pain and suffering of his people. In the midst of despair he calls for hope: "The more full of troubles and problems we are, the more bewildering life's ways, the more we must look up to the skies and hear the great news: 'A Savior is born to you.'" In the midst of powerlessness he offers courage: "Let us not be disheartened as though human realities made impossible the accomplishment of God's plans." In the midst of agony he announces the resurrection: "Those who have disappeared will reappear...Affliction...will become Easter resurrection if we join ourselves to Christ..." In the midst of violence he preaches the Beatitudes: "There are people who opt for guerrilla war, for revolution...The church's option is for the Beatitudes...Christ was sowing a moral revolution in which we human beings come to change ourselves from worldly thinking." In the midst of hatred he proclaims love: "Let us not tire of preaching love; it is the force that will overcome the world." His confidence is so strong that he can say without any ambiguity: "I simply want to be the builder of a great affirmation, the affirmation of God, who loves us and who wants to save us." As I let the words of Archbishop Romero enter more deeply into my heart I gradually come to experience that this humble but confident man becomes also for me the great affirmation of God's inexhaustible love.

LET ME NOW SPEAK about the other side of this encounter. It is my side! How can I respond when a voice, so humble but so strong, touches me deeply? This book tells me clearly to what Oscar Romero invites me. His words are a clear call to conversion and action. When Archbishop Romero first spoke the words gathered in this book, he directed himself to all the people in El Salvador, people from the left as well as people from the right, people supportive of the guerrillas as well as people in the government and the army, people who were being killed as well as their killers, the oppressed as well as the oppressors. But now after these words have been sanctified by his martyrdom they have become words for all people, and especially for the people of the United States. Now they have become words asking for a response not only from the people in El Salvador but also from us, who participate, willingly or unwillingly, knowingly or unknowingly, in the violence and destruction suffered by the Salvadorans. And who are we? Whether we want it or not, we are the rich, the powerful, the oppressors who pay the bills for the arms that kill and torture in El Salvador.

And thus Oscar Romero's words become a call to conversion. He says it loudly: "I call to everyone: Let us be converted so that Christ may look upon our faith and have mercy on us." To me, a Christian of the first world, he says without hesitation: "When one knows that financial capital, political influence, and power are worthless...that is when one begins to experience faith and conversion." To me, the rich Christian, he says: "When we speak of the church of the poor, we are simply telling the rich also: Turn your eyes to this church and concern yourselves for the poor as for yourselves." It is painful to hear these words as directed to myself, but since they come from a man as faithful as Oscar Romero, I may be able to let them come close and lead me to repentance and conversion. I am not an outsider to El Salvador's agony. I participate in it by continuing to adore the idols of "money, political interest, and national security" and by not letting the God of Jesus Christ, who became poor for my sake, guide all of my life and all of my actions. Thus I am called to confess my role in the violence that Oscar Romero condemns, to ask for forgiveness for my sins against the people who are exploited and oppressed, and to be converted.

But Oscar Romero asks for more. He asks for action that leads to justice and peace. One of the dominant themes of his sermons is the incarnation: Christ is the Word that became flesh in history. Conversion leads to engagement: "Some want to keep a gospel so disembodied that it doesn't get involved at all in the world it must save. Christ is now in history. Christ is in the womb of the people. Christ is now bringing about the new heavens and the new earth." He leaves little doubt that a true Christian must participate in the work of liberation: "Christ appeared...with the signs of liberation: shaking off oppressive yokes, bringing joy to hearts, sowing hope. And this is what God is doing now in history." Again and again Oscar Romero stresses the active nature of God's word. "We cannot separate God's word from the historical reality in which it is proclaimed...It is God's word because it enlightens, contrasts, repudiates, praises what is going on today in this society." A commitment to the word requires a commitment to history. Such a commitment challenges us to recognize, criticize, and change the unjust structures of a society that causes suffering. Such a commitment leads to conflicts and persecutions. Such a commitment can even ask of us that we give everything, even our life, for the cause of justice and peace.

ARCHBISHOP ROMERO calls to the hard service of the word. "What marks the genuine church is when the word, burning like the word of the prophets, proclaims and denounces: proclaims to the people God's wonders to be believed and venerated, and denounces the sins of those who oppose God's reign, so that they may tear those sins out of their hearts, out of their societies, out of their laws – out of the structures that oppress, that imprison, that violate the rights of God and of humanity. This is the hard service of the word." To this active service I feel called by Oscar Romero, the martyr of El Salvador. It is indeed a very great demand, but it is the demand of Jesus himself, respoken in the concrete historical context in which we live. As a Christian I am invited – yes, required – to work with all my energy for the salvation of the world. Oscar Romero makes it clear that such a work cannot be spiritualized: "All practices that disagree with the gospel must be removed if we are to save people. We must save not the soul at the hour of death but the person living in history." Thus conversion opens me to action, an action for justice and peace in the concreteness of our contemporary society.

The encounter with Oscar Romero, the humble but confident man of God calling me to conversion and action for peace and justice, was the fruit of the texts this book contains. I never met Archbishop Romero during his life. But I met him in a very special way in his words, which truly became flesh, not only through the way he lived, but also through the way he died. His life and death have given these words a unique authority. It is the authority of the compassionate shepherd, the shepherd who suffers with his people and gives his life for them. One day

Oscar Romero said to his people: "I sense that there is something new in the archdiocese. I am a man, frail and limited, and I do not know what is happening, but I do know that God knows." This spiritual intuition proved to be true. Something very new is happening in the church of Central America. Out of the anguish and agony of his people the Spirit of God is fashioning a new creation. I pray that those who will read this book and allow the words of Oscar Romero to enter into their innermost being will also sense that something new is happening in them.

Henri J. M. Nouwen

Preface

ARCHBISHOP OSCAR A. ROMERO gave his life, in the words of Pope John Paul II, "for the church and the people of his beloved country" of El Salvador. His death from an assassin's bullet on March 24, 1980, crowned a life of service as priest and bishop. During his three years as archbishop of San Salvador, he became known across the world as a fearless defender of the poor and suffering. The universities of Georgetown and Louvain gave him honorary degrees, and British parliamentarians nominated him for the Nobel Peace Prize. Yet he earned also the hatred and calumny of powerful persons in his own country – hatred that produced constant attacks on him in the national media and inevitably led to his martyrdom.

Week after week for three years, Archbishop Romero's voice rang out over El Salvador, crying out against murder and torture, exhorting his people to seek peace and forgiveness and to build a more just society. By means of the archdiocese's radio station (unless its transmissions were jammed or its plant too badly damaged from dynamite attacks) he kept a whole nation hanging on his words. It seemed that one could hardly help hearing his voice from some radio on Sunday morning, especially in the neighborhoods of the poor and in the villages of the peasants.

Oscar Romero achieved his rare eloquence not by writing polished sermons but by speaking directly to his listeners about their lives, and especially the lives of the poor, whose sufferings, he said, "touch the very heart of God." The majority of Salvadorans are poor. It was mostly the poor who filled the cathedral for his 8 A.M. Sunday Mass, and it was the poor who surrounded him on his visits to even the most isolated hamlets of his diocese. But persons of all kinds testified that he and his words strengthened their faith, and he in turn found his own faith reinforced by the people.

This selection of Archbishop Romero's thoughts is meant to enable others to know this man of faith and to experience the power of his words.

James R. Brockman, S. J.

Translator's Note

PART OF THE MATERIAL published in this book appeared in a previous volume, *The Church Is All of You* (Winston Press). The greater part of it, however, appears here for the first time in English.

The selections of Archbishop Romero's words are taken from his homilies, except where noted otherwise. When I thought the reader might be helped by looking up the entire Bible passage on which Archbishop Romero was preaching or the readings of the Mass he was celebrating, I have given the Bible references. Translations of Bible texts used in this book are my own, though I am indebted to certain traditional renderings.

J. R. B.

CHAPTER ONE

A Pilgrim Church

Let us not forget:
we are a pilgrim church,
    subject to misunderstanding,
    to persecution,
but a church that walks serene
because it bears the force of love.[1]

MARCH 14, 1977

The church's social teaching tells everyone that the Christian religion does not have a merely horizontal meaning, or a merely spiritualized meaning that overlooks the wretchedness that surrounds it. It is a looking at God, and from God at one's neighbor as a brother or sister, and an awareness that "whatever you did to one of these, you did to me."[2]

Would that social movements knew this social teaching! They would not expose themselves to failures, to shortsightedness, to a nearsightedness that sees no more than temporal things, the structures of time. As long as one does not live a conversion in one's heart, a teaching enlightened by faith to organize life according to the heart of God, all will be feeble, revolutionary, passing, violent. None of these is Christian.

MARCH 14, 1977

We will be firm in defending our rights –
but with a great love in our hearts,
because when we defend ourselves with love
   we are also seeking sinners' conversion.
That is the Christian's vengeance.[3]

JUNE 19, 1977

As Christians formed in the gospel
you have the right to organize
   and, inspired by the gospel,
to make concrete decisions.
But be careful not to betray
those evangelical, Christian, supernatural convictions
   in the company of those who seek other liberations
   that can be merely economic, temporal, political.
Even though working for liberation
   along with those who hold other ideologies,
Christians must cling to their original liberation.

JUNE 19, 1977

I speak a word of encouragement,
   for the Lord's light will always brighten these ways.
New shepherds will come,
   but always the same gospel.

JUNE 19, 1977

We must learn this invitation of Christ:
   "Those who wish to come after me
   must renounce themselves."[4]
Let them renounce themselves,

renounce their comforts,
renounce their personal opinions,
and follow only the mind of Christ,
which can lead us to death
but will surely also lead us to resurrection.

JUNE 19, 1977

One of the signs of the present time is the idea of participation, the right that all persons have to participate in the construction of their own common good.

For this reason, one of the most dangerous abuses of the present time is repression, the attitude that says, "Only we can govern, no one else; get rid of them."

Everyone can contribute much that is good, and in that way trust is achieved. The common good will not be attained by excluding people. We can't enrich the common good of our country by driving out those we don't care for. We have to try to bring out all that is good in each person and try to develop an atmosphere of trust, not with physical force, as though dealing with irrational beings, but with a moral force that draws out the good that is in everyone, especially in concerned young people.

Thus, with all contributing their own interior life, their own responsibility, their own way of being, all can build the beautiful structure of the common good, the good that we construct together and that creates conditions of kindness, of trust, of freedom, of peace.

Then we can, all of us together, build the republic – the *res publica*, the public concern – what belongs to all of us and what we all have the duty of building.

JULY 10, 1977

The Christian must work to exclude sin
  and establish God's reign.
To struggle for this is not communism.
To struggle for this is not to mix in politics.
It is simply that the gospel demands of today's Christian
  more commitment to history.

JULY 16, 1977

Pius XII said that the world must be saved from savagery
  to make it more human
  and thence to make it divine.
That is, all practices that disagree with the gospel
must be removed
  if we are to save people.
We must save not the soul at the hour of death
  but the person living in history.

JULY 16, 1977

Not just purgatory but hell awaits
  those who could have done good and did not do it.
It is the reverse
of the Beatitude that the Bible has
  for those who are saved,
  for the saints,
  "who could have done wrong and did not."[5]
Of those who are condemned it will be said:
They could have done good and did not.

JULY 16, 1977

The true protagonists of history are those who are most united with God, because with God's viewpoint they can best attend to the signs of the times, the ways of Providence, the building of history. Oh, if we only had persons of prayer among those who oversee the fate of the nation and the fate of the economy! If, instead of relying on human devices, people would rely on God and on his devices, we would have a world like the one the church dreams of, a world without injustices, a world with respect for rights, a world with generous participation by all, a world without repression, a world without torture.

JULY 17, 1977

You heard today in the first reading the accusations: "Death to that Jeremiah! He's demoralizing the soldiers and all of the people with those speeches. That man doesn't promote the people's good, but their harm."[6]

See how the accusations against the prophets of all times are the same. When the prophet bothers the consciences of the selfish, or of those who are not building with God's plans, he is a nuisance and must be eliminated, murdered, thrown into a pit, persecuted, not allowed to speak the word that annoys.

But the prophet could not tell them anything else. Read in the Bible how Jeremiah often prays to God, "Lord, take this cross away from me. I don't want to be a prophet. I feel my insides burning because I have to say things even I don't like."[7]

It's always the same. The prophet has to speak of society's sin and call to conversion, as the church is doing today in San Salvador: pointing out whatever would enthrone sin in El Salvador's history and calling sinners to be converted, just as Jeremiah did.

AUGUST 14, 1977

A humble person is one who, like the humble Mary, says, "The Powerful One has done great things in me."[8] Each of us has an individual greatness. God would not be our author if we were something worthless. You and I and all of us are worth very much, because we are creatures of God, and God has prodigally given his wonderful gifts to every person. And so the church values human beings and contends for their rights, for their freedom, for their dignity. That is an authentic church endeavor. While human rights are violated, while there are arbitrary arrests, while there are tortures, the church considers itself persecuted, it feels troubled, because the church values human beings and cannot tolerate that an image of God be trampled by persons that become brutalized by trampling on others. The church wants to make that image beautiful.

SEPTEMBER 4, 1977

Would that the many bloodstained hands in our land
    were lifted up to the Lord with horror of their stain
    to pray that he might cleanse them.
But let those who, thanks to God, have clean hands –
the children, the sick, the suffering –
lift up their innocent and suffering hands to the Lord
    like the people of Israel in Egypt.
The Lord will have pity and will say,
    as he did to Moses in Egypt,
"I have heard my people's cry of wailing."[9]
It is the prayer that God cannot fail to hear.

SEPTEMBER 18, 1977

Let us not tire of preaching love;
   it is the force that will overcome the world.
Let us not tire of preaching love.
   Though we see that waves of violence
succeed in drowning the fire of Christian love,
   love must win out; it is the only thing that can.

SEPTEMBER 25, 1977

It is not my poor word that sows hope and faith;
I am no more than God's humble echo in this people,
speaking to those chosen as God's scourges,
   who practice violence in so many ways.
But let them beware. When God no longer needs them,
he will cast them into the fire.
Let them instead be converted in time.
And to those who suffer the scourges
and do not understand the why
of the injustices and abuses:
Have faith. Give yourselves,
   will and mind and heart, entire.
God has his time.
Our missing ones are not missing to God's eyes,
and those who have taken them away are present also
   to God's justice.
For all of them,
and for a world that suffers uncertainty,
let us pray for the assurance of faith.

OCTOBER 2, 1977

It would be worthless to have an economic liberation
in which all the poor had their own houses,
      their own money,
but were all sinners,
    their hearts estranged from God.
What good would it be?
There are nations at present
that are economically and socially quite advanced,
for example those of northern Europe,
and yet how much vice and excess!

The church will always have its word to say:
conversion.
Progress will not be completed
even if we organize ideally the economy
and the political and social order of our people.
It won't be entire with that.
That will be the basis,
so that it can be completed
    by what the church pursues and proclaims:
God adored by all,
Christ acknowledged as only Savior,
deep joy of spirit
    in being at peace with God
    and with our brothers and sisters.

OCTOBER 9, 1977

How I would like to engrave this great idea
    on each one's heart:
Christianity is not a collection of truths to be believed,
    of laws to be obeyed,
    of prohibitions.
That makes it very distasteful.

Christianity is a person,
 one who loved us so much,
 one who calls for our love.
Christianity is Christ.

Do you want to know if your Christianity is genuine?
Here is the touchstone:
 Whom do you get along with?
 Who are those who criticize you?
 Who are those who do not accept you?
 Who are those who flatter you?
Know from that what Christ said once:
"I have come not to bring peace, but division."[10]
There will be division even in the same family,
because some want to live more comfortably
 by the world's principles,
 those of power and money.
But others have embraced the call of Christ
and must reject all that cannot be just in the world.

"But not a hair of your head will perish.
By your endurance you will save your lives."[11]
Let the Day of the Lord come when it will,
what matters is to endure with Christ,
 faithful to his teaching,
 not to betray him.
I pity the many turncoats,
 Christians who are now spies,
 Christians who now persecute us,
 Christians who turn away,

ashamed of their bishop and their priests.
But the firmness of those who remain faithful
    truly fills me with courage.
I tell you, brothers and sisters,
let us not be frightened.

NOVEMBER 13, 1977

The church is calling to sanity,
    to understanding,
    to love.
It does not believe in violent solutions.
The church believes in only one violence,
that of Christ,
    who was nailed to the cross.
That is how today's gospel reading shows him,
taking upon himself all the violence
    of hatred and misunderstanding,
so that we humans might forgive one another,
    love one another,
    feel ourselves brothers and sisters.[12]

NOVEMBER 20, 1977

How beautiful will be the day
when all the baptized understand
    that their work, their job,
        is a priestly work,
that just as I celebrate Mass at this altar,
so each carpenter celebrates Mass at his workbench,
and each metalworker,
each professional,
each doctor with the scalpel,

the market woman at her stand,
is performing a priestly office!
How many cabdrivers, I know, listen to this message
    there in their cabs;
you are a priest at the wheel, my friend,
    if you work with honesty,
consecrating that taxi of yours to God,
bearing a message of peace and love
    to the passengers who ride in your cab.

NOVEMBER 20, 1977

God enters the human heart by its own ways:
He enters the wise through wisdom.
He enters the simple through simplicity.

NOVEMBER 25, 1977

When we preach the Lord's word,
we decry not only the injustices of the social order.
We decry every sin that is night, that is darkness:
    drunkenness, gluttony, lust, adultery, abortion,
    everything that is the reign of iniquity and sin.
Let them all disappear from our society.

NOVEMBER 27, 1977

We cannot segregate God's word
from the historical reality in which it is proclaimed.
It would not then be God's word.
It would be history,
it would be a pious book,
    a Bible that is just a book in our library.
It becomes God's word

because it vivifies,
enlightens, contrasts,
repudiates, praises
    what is going on today in this society.

NOVEMBER 27, 1977

We have never preached violence,
except the violence of love,
which left Christ nailed to a cross,
    the violence that we must each do to ourselves
    to overcome our selfishness
    and such cruel inequalities among us.
The violence we preach is not the violence of the sword,
    the violence of hatred.
It is the violence of love,
    of brotherhood,
the violence that wills to beat weapons
into sickles for work.

NOVEMBER 27, 1977

Brothers and sisters, at this moment
Christ the Redeemer needs human suffering,
    needs the pain of those holy mothers who suffer,
    needs the anguish of prisoners who suffer tortures.
Blessed are those who are chosen to continue on earth
the great injustice suffered by Christ,
who keeps on saving the world.
Let us turn that injustice into redemption.[13]

DECEMBER 1, 1977

I assure you
   that today the holy suffering of so many homes
   that suffer unjust orphanhood
is also a suffering that nourishes,
that injects life, love of God,
   into this church that is preaching hope,
   preaching that we must not despair,
that days of justice must come,
days in which God will triumph over human evil,
over diabolical human wickedness.

DECEMBER 1, 1977

"For those who love God,
all things work for their good."[14]
There is no misfortune,
   there are no catastrophes,
   there are no sorrows, however extraordinary,
   that cannot become crowns of glory and of hope
when suffered with love for God.

DECEMBER 1, 1977

Do not let the serpent of rancor nest in your hearts.
There is no greater misfortune than a vindictive heart,
even though it be turned against those
who have tortured your children,
   against the criminal hands
   that have placed them among the missing.
Do not hate.

DECEMBER 1, 1977

Brothers and sisters, the church is not mistaken.
The church awaits with certainty the hour of redemption.
   Those who have disappeared will reappear.
   The sorrows of these mothers will be turned into Easter.
The affliction of this people,
   which knows not where it goes amid so much affliction,
will become Easter resurrection
if we join ourselves to Christ
and hope in him.

DECEMBER 1, 1977

Even when all despaired
   at the hour when Christ was dying on the cross,
Mary, serene,
   awaited the hour of the resurrection.
Mary is the symbol
   of the people who suffer oppression and injustice.
Theirs is the calm suffering
   that awaits the resurrection.
It is Christian suffering,
   the suffering of the church,
   which does not accept the present injustices
   but awaits without rancor the moment
   when the Risen One will return
   to give us the redemption we await.

DECEMBER 1, 1977

I cry out against injustice,
   but only to say to the unjust:
Be converted!
I cry out in the name of suffering,

of those who suffer injustice,
 but only to say to the criminals:
Be converted!
Do not be wicked!

DECEMBER 1, 1977

We human beings cannot produce our land's liberation.
We Salvadorans are unable to save our country
with our own human powers.
But if we hope for a liberation to come from Christ,
 the Redeemer,
then we can.
This is the church's hope.
This is why I preach much faith in Christ.
He died to pay for all injustices
 and rose to bury in his tomb all evil
 and become the redemption of all those who suffer.
He is hope and eternal life.

DECEMBER 1, 1977

A religion of Sunday Mass but of unjust weeks
 does not please the Lord.
A religion of much praying but with hypocrisy in the heart
 is not Christian.
A church that sets itself up only to be well off,
 to have a lot of money and comfort,
but that forgets to protest injustices,
 would not be the true church of our divine Redeemer.

DECEMBER 4, 1977

How arid we human beings are
when the Holy Spirit is not in us!
How cruel people become
when animated not by God's Spirit
but by the spirit of getting along in the world!
It pains my heart deeply
    to know how our people are tortured,
    how the rights of God's image are trampled.
That should not be.
Without God, humans are wild beasts.
Without God, they are deserts.
Their hearts have no blossoms of love.
They are only the perverse persecutors
of their brothers and sisters.
That is why there are hearts
capable of betraying others,
    of informing on them, not caring
    that they are led away to be tortured and killed.[15]

DECEMBER 5, 1977

To be a Christian now means to have the courage
to preach the true teaching of Christ
    and not be afraid of it, not be silent out of fear
    and preach something easy that won't cause problems.
To be a Christian in this hour means
    to have the courage that the Holy Spirit gives
in the sacrament of confirmation,
    to be valiant soldiers of Christ the King,
    to make his teaching prevail,
    to reach hearts and proclaim to them the courage
that one must have to defend God's law.

DECEMBER 5, 1977

Beginning with me, the bishop,
may this morning be for us a renewal of our Holy Spirit,
of the courage that we must have as Christians.
And, if necessary, may confirmation
  become for us a sacrament of martyrdom.
May we too be ready to give our lives for Christ
and not betray him with the cowardice
  of today's false Christians.

DECEMBER 5, 1977

This is why the church has great conflicts:
  It accuses of sin.
It says to the rich:
  Do not sin by misusing your money.
It says to the powerful:
  Do not misuse your political influence.
  Do not misuse your weaponry.
  Do not misuse your power.
  Don't you see that is a sin?
It says to sinful torturers:
  Do not torture.
  You are sinning.
  You are doing wrong.
  You are establishing the reign of hell on earth.

DECEMBER 8, 1977

The church, with its message, with its word,
will meet a thousand obstacles,
  just as the river encounters boulders, rocks, chasms.
No matter;

the river carries a promise:
"I will be with you to the end of the ages"
    and: "The gates of hell shall not prevail"[16]
against the will of the Lord.

DECEMBER 8, 1977

It is very easy to be servants of the word without disturbing the world: a very spiritualized word, a word without any commitment to history, a word that can sound in any part of the world because it belongs to no part of the world. A word like that creates no problems, starts no conflicts.

What starts conflicts and persecutions, what marks the genuine church, is the word that, burning like the word of the prophets, proclaims and accuses: proclaims to the people God's wonders to be believed and venerated, and accuses of sin those who oppose God's reign, so that they may tear that sin out of their hearts, out of their societies, out of their laws – out of the structures that oppress, that imprison, that violate the rights of God and of humanity.

This is the hard service of the word.

But God's Spirit goes with the prophet, with the preacher, for he is Christ, who keeps on proclaiming his reign to the people of all times.[17]

DECEMBER 10, 1977

One day, there will be no more Masses,
    no more need of temporal priests,
because all of us,
    through the labors of priests, of bishops,
    of catechists, of lay ministers of the word,
    of all God's priestly people,

will have achieved humanity's incorporation into Christ,
and Christ will be the one priest,
formed in his historical and eternal fullness
  by all of us who in the course of history
  have made with him one sole priesthood,
  one sole offertory, one sole Mass
  that will last eternally to sing God's glory.
This is the destiny, the objective
for which we priests work in history.
There, my brother priests, in everlasting glory
along with all of our people, our people glorified,
we shall feel the boundless satisfaction
of having worked with Christ
  to make humanity God's living temple,
the living image of God's Spirit in eternity.

DECEMBER 10, 1977

Israel's history is a theocratic history. God writes it with his
prophets, with his human beings, with his deeds. The deeds,
Israel's historical events, have a prophetic meaning. What God
does to Israel, he wants to do with all peoples. Other peoples
must learn from the Bible, from sacred history. It is the paradigm
of all histories.

DECEMBER 11, 1977

A nation is built upon God's designs, and my country's true vocation is to be a land of salvation.

    The true vocation of Salvadorans is that we should one day
become God's kingdom, not just baptized in name but actually
Christians, committed to make of our homes, our estates, our
farms, our ways, our laws, a structure of salvation, where Salva-

dorans may feel themselves truly realized as Christians, able to adore their God with freedom, complete freedom, able to proclaim the integral religion that God bids them proclaim, to meet together to reflect on his word without fear of surveillance or evil reports, to love God while meeting in their chapels without being suspected of doing something else.

This is the freedom the church preaches.

DECEMBER 11, 1977

CHAPTER TWO

A History of Salvation

The church's task in each country
is to make of each country's individual history
   a history of salvation.

DECEMBER 11, 1977

What beautiful coffee groves,
   what fine cane and cotton fields,
   what farms, what lands God has given us!
Nature is so beautiful!

But we see it groan
   under oppression,
   under wickedness,
   under injustice,
   under abuse,
and the church feels its pain.

Nature looks for a liberation
that will not be mere material well-being
but God's act of power.

God will free nature from sinful human hands,
and along with the redeemed it will sing a hymn of joy
   to God the Liberator.

DECEMBER 11, 1977

Mary and the church in Latin America are marked by poverty.
Vatican Council II says that Mary stands out
among the poor who await redemption from God.
Mary appears in the Bible
    as the expression of poverty, of humility,
    of one who needs everything from God.
When she comes to America,
her intimate, motherly converse is with an Indian,
an outcast, a poor man.[18]
Mary's dialog in America begins with a sign of poverty,
    poverty that is hunger for God,
    poverty that is joy of independence.
    Poverty is freedom.
    Poverty is needing others,
needing brothers and sisters,
supporting one another so as to help one another.
This is what Mary means
and what the church means in Latin America.

If at some time the church betrayed its spirit of poverty,
    then it was unfaithful to the gospel,
which meant it to be distinct from the powers of the earth,
    not depending on the money that makes humans happy,
    but depending on the power of Christ,
    on God's power.
That is its greatness.

DECEMBER 12, 1977

Our people sense that Mary is part of our people's soul.
    All Latin American peoples feel this.
No one has entered so deeply into our people's heart as Mary.
She is the image, the likeness,
    of a church that wants to be present with the gospel's light

in the civilizations of the world's peoples,
as God wants her to be,
 in their social, economic, and political transformation.

DECEMBER 12, 1977

Faith consists in accepting God
 without asking him to account for things
 according to our standard.
Faith consists in reacting before God as Mary did:
 I don't understand it, Lord,
 but let it be done in me according to your word.

DECEMBER 18, 1977

Who knows if the one whose hands are bloodied
with Father Grande's murder,
 or the one who shot Father Navarro,
 if those who have killed, who have tortured,
 who have done so much evil, are listening to me?[19]
Listen, there in your criminal hideout,
perhaps already repentant,
 you too are called to forgiveness.

DECEMBER 18, 1977

When we struggle for human rights,
 for freedom,
 for dignity,
when we feel that it is a ministry of the church
to concern itself for those who are hungry,
for those who are deprived,
we are not departing from God's promise.
He comes to free us from sin,

and the church knows that sin's consequences
are all such injustices and abuses.
The church knows it is saving the world
when it undertakes to speak also of such things.

DECEMBER 18, 1977

It is not an advantage of great value to be well off on this earth
by betraying Christ and his church.

It is an advantage that is very cheap, one that is to be left behind with this life.

It is terrible to hear from the lips of Christ: "Depart from me,
wicked, accursed ones. I do not know you. I will be ashamed of
whoever is ashamed of me."[20]

DECEMBER 19, 1977

Let us not measure the church by the number of its members
    or by its material buildings.
The church has built many houses of worship,
    many seminaries,
    many buildings that have been taken from her.
They have been stolen
    and turned into libraries
    and barracks
    and markets
    and other things.
That doesn't matter.
The material walls here will be left behind in history.
What matters is you, the people,
    your hearts.
    God's grace giving you God's truth and life.
Don't measure yourselves by your numbers.
Measure yourselves by the sincerity of heart

with which you follow the truth and light
of our divine Redeemer.

DECEMBER 19, 1977

With Christ, God has injected himself into history. With the
birth of Christ, God's reign is now inaugurated in human time.

On this night, as every year for twenty centuries, we recall
that God's reign is now in this world and that Christ has inaugurated the fullness of time. His birth attests that God is now
marching with us in history, that we do not go alone.

Humans long for peace, for justice, for a reign of divine law,
for something holy, for what is far from earth's realities. We can
have such a hope, not because we ourselves are able to construct
the realm of happiness that God's holy words proclaim, but because the builder of a reign of justice, of love, and of peace is
already in the midst of us.

DECEMBER 25, 1977

Let us not be disheartened,
    even when the horizon of history grows dim and closes in,
as though human realities made impossible
the accomplishment of God's plans.
God makes use even of human errors,
    even of human sins,
    so as to make rise over the darkness what Isaiah spoke of.
One day prophets will sing
    not only the return from Babylon
    but our full liberation.
"The people that walked in darkness have seen a great light.
They walk in lands of shadows,
    but a light has shone forth."[21]

DECEMBER 25, 1977

For the church, the many abuses
of human life, liberty, and dignity
are a heartfelt suffering.
The church, entrusted with the earth's glory,
believes that in each person is the Creator's image
    and that everyone who tramples it offends God.
As holy defender of God's rights and of his images,
the church must cry out.
It takes as spittle in its face,
    as lashes on its back,
    as the cross in its passion,
    all that human beings suffer,
even though they be unbelievers.
They suffer as God's images.
There is no dichotomy between man and God's image.
    Whoever tortures a human being,
    whoever abuses a human being,
    whoever outrages a human being
abuses God's image,
and the church takes as its own
that cross, that martyrdom.

DECEMBER 31, 1977

I am glad that a serious examination of living the gospel
    is being made among Protestants.
There is conflict – God be blessed.
When a sore spot is touched,
    there is conflict, there is pain.
And Protestantism is putting its hand on the sore spot.
It is saying that one cannot be a true Protestant,
a true follower of the gospel,

if one does not draw from the gospel
    all the conclusions it contains for this earth,
that one cannot live a gospel that is too angelical,
    a gospel of compliance,
    a gospel that is not dynamic peace,
    a gospel that is not of demanding dimensions
in regard to temporal matters also.

DECEMBER 31, 1977

As the magi from the East followed their star
and found Jesus,
    who filled their hearts with boundless joy,
let us too,
    even in hours of uncertainty, of shadows, of darkness
    like those the magi had,
not fail to follow that star,
    the star of our faith.[22]

JANUARY 8, 1978 (EPIPHANY)

Peace is not the product of terror or fear.
Peace is not the silence of cemeteries.
Peace is not the silent result of violent repression.
Peace is the generous, tranquil contribution of all
    to the good of all.
Peace is dynamism. Peace is generosity.
It is right and it is duty.
In it each one has a place in this beautiful family,
which the Epiphany brightens for us with God's light.

JANUARY 8, 1978

Defense of human rights, equality, and freedom is not only a matter of policy. It is a matter of policy, but of policy rooted in the gospel. The gospel is the great defender and proclaimer of all the great fundamental rights of the person.

The gospel roots of equality will not disappear even when political expediencies disappear. Let us suppose that tomorrow it is no longer expedient for the United States to defend human rights in El Salvador. Humanly speaking, the policy may fail.

But the gospel will not fail. It will always cry out for human freedom and human dignity, even in the worst conditions of persecution.

JANUARY 8, 1978

I ask you faithful people who listen to me with love and devotion to pardon me for saying this, but it gives me more pleasure that my enemies listen to me.

I know that the reason they listen to me is that I bear them a message of love. I don't hate them. I don't want revenge. I wish them no harm.

I beg them to be converted, to come to be happy with the happiness that you have. Like the son in the parable who was always with his father, you possess the joy of your faith.[23]

JANUARY 15, 1978

God wants to save us in a people. He does not want to save us in isolation. And so today's church more than ever is accentuating the idea of being a people.

The church therefore experiences conflicts, because it does not want a mass; it wants a people. A mass is a heap of persons, the drowsier the better, the more compliant the better.

The church rejects communism's slander that it is the opium

of the people. It has no intention of being the people's opium.
Those that create drowsy masses are others.

The church wants to rouse men and women to the true meaning of being a people. What is a people? A people is a community of persons where all cooperate for the common good.

JANUARY 15, 1978

A society's or political community's reason for being
    is not the security of the state
but the human person.
Christ said, "Man is not for the sabbath;
    the sabbath is for man."[24]
He puts human beings as the objective
of all laws and all institutions.
Humans are not for the state;
    the state is for them.

JANUARY 15, 1978

This is the mission entrusted to the church,
    a hard mission:
to uproot sins from history,
to uproot sins from the political order,
to uproot sins from the economy,
to uproot sins wherever they are.
    What a hard task!
It has to meet conflicts amid so much selfishness,
so much pride,
so much vanity,
so many who have enthroned the reign of sin among us.

The church must suffer for speaking the truth,
    for pointing out sin,

for uprooting sin.
No one wants to have a sore spot touched,
and therefore a society with so many sores twitches
when someone has the courage to touch it
and say: "You have to treat that.
    You have to get rid of that.
    Believe in Christ.
    Be converted."

JANUARY 15, 1978

The day when all of us Salvadorans escape
    from that heap of less-human conditions
and as persons and nation
live in more-human conditions,
    not only of merely economic development,
but of the kind that lifts us up to faith,
to adoration of only one God,
    that day will know our people's real development.

JANUARY 15, 1978

We respect the temporal power,
    but we do want to create in the people's consciousness
    a feeling of being a people, not a mass.
We seek the development of individuals
and a well-being that violates no one's rights
but consists of love and faith between persons,
between sons and daughters of the Father of all.

JANUARY 15, 1978

In general, education in our Latin American countries is directed toward the desire to have more, whereas today's youth demand rather to be more, to realize themselves through service and love.

Let us not develop an education that creates in the mind of the student a hope of becoming rich and having the power to dominate. That does not correspond to the time we live in.

Let us form in the heart of the child and the young person the lofty ideal of loving, of preparing oneself to serve and to give oneself to others.

Anything else would be education for selfishness, and we want to escape the selfishness that is precisely the cause of the great malaise of our societies.

The church must propose an education that makes people agents of their own development, protagonists of history, not a passive, compliant mass, but human beings able to display their intelligence, their creativity, their desire for the common service of the nation. Education must recognize that the development of the individual and of peoples is the "advancement of each and all from less-human to more-human conditions."[25]

JANUARY 22, 1978

When Christ appeared in those lands,
   curing the sick,
   raising the dead,
   preaching to the poor,
   bringing hope to the peoples,
something began on earth like when a stone is cast
   into a quiet lake and starts ripples

that finally reach the farthest shores.
Christ appeared in Zebulun and Naphtali
  with the signs of liberation:
  shaking off oppressive yokes,
  bringing joy to hearts,
  sowing hope.[26]
And this is what God is doing now in history.

JANUARY 22, 1978

A preaching that does not point out sin
  is not the preaching of the gospel.
A preaching that makes sinners feel good,
  so that they become entrenched in their sinful state,
    betrays the gospel's call.
A preaching that does not discomfit sinners
  but lulls them in their sin
leaves Zebulun and Naphtali
  in the shadow of death.[27]

A preaching that awakens,
a preaching that enlightens —
  as when a light turned on
  awakens and of course annoys a sleeper —
that is the preaching of Christ, calling:
  Wake up! Be converted!
That is the church's authentic preaching.
Naturally, such preaching must meet conflict,
  must spoil what is miscalled prestige,
  must disturb,
  must be persecuted.
It cannot get along with the powers of darkness and sin.

JANUARY 22, 1978

"In your midst I will leave a poor and humble people,"
  says today's passage from Zephaniah.[28]
That is what the church wants:
  a humble people,
  a people that follows Christ:
  a remnant.
It is not great crowds that should excite us,
  but the authenticity,
  the quality of Christians,
  their sincerity in seeking Christ.

JANUARY 29, 1978

The world does not say: blessed are the poor.

The world says: blessed are the rich. You are worth as much as you have.

But Christ says: wrong. Blessed are the poor, for theirs is the kingdom of heaven,[29] because they do not put their trust in what is so transitory.

JANUARY 29, 1978

Blessed are the poor,
  for they know that their riches are in the One
who being rich made himself poor
in order to enrich us with his poverty,
  teaching us the Christian's true wisdom.

JANUARY 29, 1978

The Beatitudes are not something we can understand fully, and that is why there are young people especially who think that the love of the Beatitudes is not going to bring about a better world and who opt for violence, for guerrilla war, for revolution.

The church will never make that its path. Let it be clear, I repeat, that the church does not choose those ways of violence and that whatever is said to that effect is slander. The church's option is for what Christ says in the Beatitudes.

I am not surprised, though, that this is not understood. Young people especially are impatient and want a better world right away. But Christ, who preached this message twenty centuries ago, knew that he was sowing a long-term moral revolution in which we human beings come to change ourselves from worldly thinking.

JANUARY 29, 1978

There is one rule by which to judge if God is near us
    or is far away —
the rule that God's word is giving us today:
everyone concerned for the hungry, the naked, the poor,
    for those who have vanished in police custody,
    for the tortured,
    for prisoners,
    for all flesh that suffers,
has God close at hand.[30]

FEBRUARY 5, 1978

The guarantee of one's prayer
    is not in saying a lot of words.
The guarantee of one's petition is very easy to know:

how do I treat the poor?
  Because that is where God is.
The degree to which you approach them,
and the love with which you approach them,
or the scorn with which you approach them –
  that is how you approach your God.
What you do to them, you do to God.
The way you look at them is the way you look at God.

FEBRUARY 5, 1978

Dear poor people, dispossessed people, you who lack house and food, your very dignity demands your advancement.

It is a pity that you, the poor, should not respect yourselves as you ought and that you try to drown – in drink, in bad habits, in excess – a dignity that could be God's light, God's presence on earth.

We do not praise poverty for itself. We praise it as the sign, as the sacrament, of God in the world.

A sacrament must be respected, because it is a sign of God. The poor must respect themselves, must better themselves, must work to the extent that the scope of their economic and social powers enables them.

FEBRUARY 5, 1978

"I came to you weak and fearful."[31]
God knows how hard it was for me also
  to come here to the capital.
How timid I have felt before you,
except for the support that you,
  as church, have given me.
You have made your bishop a sign of Christianity.

FEBRUARY 5, 1978

"When I came to announce to you the testimony of God,
    I did so not with lofty eloquence or wisdom.
I never cared to know anything among you
    but Jesus Christ, and him crucified."[32]
I would not want human wisdom and eloquence
    to intervene in my poor speech,
because then I would be giving you the world's vanity
    and not the wisdom of the Crucified.

FEBRUARY 5, 1978

What is my word, what is human wisdom
    but a noise that reaches the outer ear?
But from that ear to the heart lies a road
    that only God can travel.
Blessed the preacher
    who does not put his trust
in the noise of his own words,
    even though they come wrapped in great human wisdom.

FEBRUARY 5, 1978

When the church decries revolutionary violence, it cannot forget that institutionalized violence also exists, and that the desperate violence of oppressed persons is not overcome with one-sided laws, with weapons, or with superior force.

Instead, as the pope says, revolutionary violence must be prevented by courageous self-sacrifice, by giving up many comforts. As long as there is not greater justice among us, there will always be outbreaks of revolution.

The church does not approve or justify bloody revolution and cries of hatred. But neither can it condemn them while it sees no attempt to remove the causes that produce that ailment in our society.

This is the church's stand, one that makes it suffer terrible conflicts, but one that also makes it feel faithful to God's justice and to the gospel of Jesus Christ.

FEBRUARY 12, 1978

We should not wonder that a church
    has a lot of cross to bear.
Otherwise, it will not have a lot of resurrection.
An accommodating church,
    a church that seeks prestige
    without the pain of the cross,
    is not the authentic church of Jesus Christ.

FEBRUARY 19, 1978

Let them steal our material churches;
    the church's history is full of that.
That's not why the church is on earth.
The church is something different, says Christ.
The church seeks adorers of God in Spirit and in truth,
and that can be done
    under a tree, on a mountain, by the sea.[33]
Wherever there is a sincere heart that seeks God sincerely,
    there is true religion.
This, my friends, scandalizes many
    because many have wanted to tie the church
    to these material things.
They call this prestige,

they call it faithfulness to their traditions.
But it can be a betrayal of the church's truth.
God is Spirit
and does not need the powers and things of earth.
He seeks sincerity in the heart.

FEBRUARY 26, 1978

CHAPTER THREE

The Idol of Self

Holy Week is a call to follow Christ's austerities,
   the only legitimate violence,
the violence that he does to himself
   and that he invites us to do to ourselves:
"Let those who would follow me deny themselves,"
   be violent to themselves,
repress in themselves the outbursts of pride,
   kill in their hearts the outbursts of greed,
of avarice, of conceit, of arrogance.[34]
   Let them kill it in their hearts.
This is what must be killed,
   this is the violence that must be done,
so that out of it a new person may arise,
   the only one who can build
a new civilization:
   a civilization of love.

MARCH 19, 1978

We must overturn so many idols,
   the idol of self first of all,
so that we can be humble,
   and only from our humility

can learn to be redeemers,
can learn to work together
in the way the world really needs.
Liberation that raises a cry against others
is no true liberation.
Liberation that means revolutions of hate and violence
and takes the lives of others
or abases the dignity of others
cannot be true liberty.
True liberty does violence to self
and, like Christ,
who disregarded that he was sovereign,
becomes a slave to serve others.

MARCH 23, 1978

People of our time,
anguished about so many problems,
deprived of hope,
seeking paradise on this earth:
Seek it not here,
seek it in Christ arisen.
Let us find in him relief for our afflictions,
for our worries,
for our anguish;
and in him let us place our hopes.

MARCH 26, 1978

Christ would not be Redeemer
if he had not concerned himself with giving food
to the crowds that were hungry,

if he had not given light to the eyes of the blind,
if he had not felt sorrow for the forsaken crowds
that had no one to love them, no one to help them.
Christianity cares about human development,
    about the political and social aspects of life.
Redemption would not be complete
if it did not consider these aspects
    of the Christ who chose in fact to be an example
    of one oppressed under a powerful empire
and under a ruling class of his people
that savaged his reputation and honor
and left him on a cross.

MARCH 26, 1978

The church cannot be deaf or mute
before the entreaty of millions of persons
who cry out for liberation,
    persons oppressed by a thousand slaveries.
But the church tells them
what is the true liberty they must seek:
    the freedom that Christ began on earth
    when he rose and burst the chains
    of sin, of death, and of hell.
It is to be like Christ, free of sin,
    to be truly free, with true liberation.

Those who put their faith in the Risen One
and work for a world more just,
who protest against the injustices
of the present system,

against the abuses of unjust authorities,
against the wrongfulness of humans exploiting humans;
all those who begin their struggle
with the resurrection of the great Liberator –
they alone are authentic Christians.

MARCH 26, 1978

I want to express thanks publicly for the strength
    that I receive from the prayers of so many.
Nothing for me is more beautiful
than to hear, "We are praying for you.
You are not alone.
We are with you in our prayer!"
God be blessed! Thank you!
And I say to you, brothers and sisters:
Let us pray for those who are weak.
Let us pray for those who betray.
Let us pray for those who are ashamed of our faith.
Let us pray for our poor brothers and sisters
    who doubt even the bishop's sincerity.
Let us pray that we line up as Christians,
even in the perilous risks of our mission.
We must be firm in what is to be preached,
and, like those first Christians,
at times we shall have to say:
    "We must obey God rather than men."[35]
And from God we'll get the power
    to proclaim the teaching that is one and true.

APRIL 2, 1978

A Christian's authenticity is shown in difficult hours. By Christian, I mean every member of God's people, whether lay person, religious, priest, bishop, or pope. And by difficult hour, I mean those circumstances in which following the gospel supposes a multitude of ruptures with the tranquility of an order that has been set up against or apart from the gospel.

I call it a difficult hour because it is very hard to live in it as a genuine follower of the only Lord. It is much easier to keep on following the many easy lords set up as idols of the moment: money, power, prestige, and so on. How easy it is then to make religion a lovely fantasy created from a false interpretation of the gospel or of the church's teaching. Those adorers of idols even go so far as to disparage with slanderous and pernicious criticism those who have the courage to remind them of the true interpretation of Christ's teaching and of their need for conversion.

And so conflict arises. There is talk of "confusion." The blame for the disorder is put on "subversive sermons." Attempts are made to isolate the voice that cries out in the name of the Lord. The church's teaching power is likened to a popular democracy, as though the number of those who speak were worth more than the rightness of what is said, and it is forgotten that mediocrity will always be majority and the courage of authenticity, minority. Recall "the wide way" and "the narrow way" of the gospel.

How necessary in this difficult hour is a conscience docile to the Lord's truth. In this difficult hour more than ever is there need for prayer united with a genuine will to be converted, prayer that out of intimacy with God cuts one off from the confused clamor of life's shallow expediencies, a will to be converted that is not afraid to lose prestige or privilege, or to change a way of thinking when it is seen that Christ insists on a new way of thinking more in keeping with his gospel.

I believe that for our archdiocese a difficult hour is here and is putting to the test the Christian authenticity of all of us who make up this local church. We should not be surprised, then, that in this test of authenticity not all that glistens is gold. But at the same time we should intensely rejoice that this moment of Christian hazard is revealing that we have much fine metal, which comes out of the crucible with greater excellence.

It is in difficult hours that the church grows in authenticity. Blest be God for this difficult hour in our archdiocese. Let us be worthy of it.[36]

APRIL 9, 1978

A church that doesn't provoke any crises,
a gospel that doesn't unsettle,
a word of God that doesn't get under anyone's skin,
a word of God that doesn't touch the real sin
    of the society in which it is being proclaimed –
what gospel is that?
Very nice, pious considerations
    that don't bother anyone,
that's the way many would like preaching to be.
Those preachers who avoid every thorny matter
    so as not to be harassed,
    so as not to have conflicts and difficulties,
do not light up the world they live in.
They don't have Peter's courage, who told that crowd
where the bloodstained hands still were
that had killed Christ:
    "You killed him!"[37]
Even though the charge could cost him his life as well,

he made it.
The gospel is courageous;
it's the good news
    of him who came to take away the world's sins.

APRIL 16, 1978

We must also mourn this week the death of two policemen. They are our brothers.

In cases of abuse and violence, my voice has never been one-sided. With Christ's compassion I have stood by the side of the dead, of the victims, of the sufferers. I ask that we pray for them, and we join with their families in their sorrow.

I declare that two policemen killed are two more victims of the injustice of our system, which I condemned last Sunday. Among its worst crimes is that it pits our poor against one another; policemen and workers or peasants, they all belong to the class of the poor. It is evil of the system to pit poor against poor. Two policemen killed are two poor men who are victims of others, also poor perhaps; and in any case they are victims of that god Moloch, insatiable for power and money. As long as he maintains his state of affairs, he cares not about the peasant's life, or the policeman's, or the soldier's; he only struggles to defend a system full of sin.

APRIL 30, 1978

I believe that our church in San Salvador
    is giving the reason for its hope,
because it does not put its hope in power or money
    but in the source of its hope,
        which is Christ crucified.[38]
Its faithfulness to the gospel is its hope;

its hope is in being faithful to God.
I tell my beloved priests,
  the religious communities,
  the Catholic schools,
  the parishes,
  the grassroots communities:
Don't be led astray
  either by the allure of power and money
  or by following false ideologies.
True hope is not found there either.
True hope is not found
  in a revolution of violence and bloodshed,
and hope is not found in money and power –
  neither on the left nor on the right.
The hope that we must account for
  and that makes us speak with valor
is found in Christ, who reigns even after death,
  even after murderous death.
And with him reign all who have preached
  his justice, his love, his hope, his peace.

APRIL 30, 1978

Those marvelous media of communication – the newspapers, the radio, television, the movies – where ideas are communicated to large masses of people, are often means of confusion.

These instruments, formers of public opinion, are often manipulated by material interests and thus become instruments to maintain an unjust state of affairs through falsehood and confusion.

There is a lack of respect for one of the most sacred rights of the human person, the right to be well informed, the right to the truth.

Each one must defend this right for himself or herself by
being critical in using the media. Not everything in the newspapers, not everything in the movies or on television, not everything heard on the radio is true. Often it is just the opposite,
a lie.

MAY 7, 1978

Money is good,
   but selfish persons have made it bad and sinful.
Power is good,
   but abuse by humans has made it something to fear.
All has been created by God,
   but humans have subjected it to sin.
And so Christ's ascension proclaims
    that the whole creation
    will also be redeemed in him,
because he will give the meaning
    of all that God has created,
and at the end of time
    (in this will consist the final judgment)
he will place at God's feet
    the great adjudication of good and evil.
Evil will be eliminated definitively
    and good will be taken up
in the eternal glorification of Christ.
The Lord's ascension also marks the glorification
    of the universe.
The universe rejoices, money rejoices, power rejoices,
    all material things –
    farms and estates, everything –
rejoice because the day will come when the Supreme Judge

will redeem from sin, from slavery, from shame,
all that God has created
    and that humans are using for sin,
    for affront against their fellows.
The redemption is already decreed,
    and in his power God has raised up Christ our Lord.
Christ gone up to heaven is a witness to final justice.

MAY 7, 1978

Even when they call us mad,
when they call us subversives and communists
and all the epithets they put on us,
we know that we only preach
the subversive witness of the Beatitudes,
which have turned everything upside down
to proclaim blessed the poor,
    blessed the thirsting for justice,
    blessed the suffering.

MAY 11, 1978

It will always be Pentecost in the church,
    provided the church lets the beauty of the Holy Spirit
    shine forth from her countenance.
When the church ceases to let her strength
rest on the power from above –
    which Christ promised her
    and which he gave her on that day –
and when the church leans rather on the weak forces

of the power or wealth of this earth,
then the church ceases to be newsworthy.

The church will be fair to see,
perennially young,
attractive in every age,
as long as she is faithful to the Spirit that floods her
and she reflects that Spirit
   through her communities,
   through her pastors,
   through her very life.

MAY 14, 1978

This is the true God,
   the God experienced,
   the God of Moses,
   the God of history,
who not only saves in Israel's history
   but saves in El Salvador's history,
and who has set up a church
   to proclaim faith in the true God
   and to purify history of sin
   and to sanctify history
in order to make it the vehicle of salvation.

This is what the church wants in El Salvador:
   to make of our nation's history
   not a history of ruin,
   not a history of atheism,
   not a history of abuses and injustices,

but a history that fits the ideals of God,
   who loves Salvadorans.

If Moses had been a Salvadoran in 1978,
   he would have heard from the burning bush
the same voice of Yahweh that he heard when God
   sent him to take the people
out of Pharaoh's tyranny:
"I am the God who is with you."[39]
Let us fill ourselves with great trust today,
   when the church invites us
to go to the sources of our hope and of our religion
   to encounter the true God,
the God who loves us, his family, as a father.

MAY 21, 1978

Faith is what a child has
   when its father puts out his hands
and says, "Jump!"
   and the child leaps into space
with the assurance that its father's hands
   won't let it fall.
This is faith.
   It's what Christ says,
"Those who believe in me
   will not be condemned."[40]
Those who surrender,
   those who don't distrust,
who even in the hardest times believe and hope,
   will not be condemned.
But those who don't believe,
   those who won't leap into Christ's arms
because they are more anchored to their earthly things,

those who don't believe,
those who don't trust in God,
those who don't believe God goes with our history
and is going to save us
are already condemned.
Their life is already a hell.

M AY   2 1 ,   1 9 7 8

Solidarity in Suffering[41]

Three men abducted; four victims of a tragic air accident; two peasants murdered after a demonstration: in recent days these are the expressive emblem of human suffering made more tragic by human wickedness.

Suffering will always be. It is a heritage of the first sin and a consequence of the other sins that God permits, even after the redemption. But the redemption converts them into power of salvation when suffering is undergone in union of faith, hope, and love with the Redeemer's divine suffering and cross. Suffering is the shadow of God's hand, which blesses and pardons; and suffering unites people in solidarity and draws them near to God.

But one could say of suffering what the Lord said of scandal: "Scandal indeed must come, but woe to the one through whom scandal comes!"[42]

Suffering is something inherent to our very nature, but to cause to suffer is criminal. Only God, author and Lord of life and of humans' happiness, has the right to take away life, or to measure, with due love and wisdom, his children's capacity to be purified in the crucible of suffering and made worthy of bliss. Every hand that touches the life, liberty, dignity, tranquility, or happiness of persons, families, or peoples is sacrilegious and criminal. All bloodshed, all suffering, every injury caused to an-

other person becomes an echo of God's curse before the crime
of Cain: "What have you done? Your brother's blood is crying
out to me from the ground. You are under a curse."[43]

MAY 26, 1978

Today the idols of the Corinthians no longer exist: idols of
gold, figures of animals, of goddesses, of stars and suns.[44] Today
other idols exist, which we have often spoken of.

If Christians are nourished in the eucharistic communion,
where their faith tells them they are united to Christ's life, how
can they live as idolaters of money, idolaters of power, selfish
idolaters of themselves? How can a Christian who receives holy
communion be an idolater?

My dear brothers and sisters, there are many who receive
communion and are idolaters. In our twentieth century, this
very year, St. Paul could say to many Christians of San Salvador
and to many communities that are reflecting on these words: If
you truly believe that Christ is present and that you are united
with him at the moment of communion, how is it possible for
you afterwards to live so immorally, so selfishly, so unjustly, so
idolatrously? How is it possible for you to put your trust more in
the things of earth than in the power of Christ, who becomes
present in the great sacrifice?

MAY 28, 1978

How beautiful is the Mass,
    especially when celebrated in a cathedral filled
    like ours on Sundays,
or even when celebrated simply
in village chapels with people full of faith,
who know that Christ, the King of Glory, Eternal Priest,

is gathering together all that we bring him from the week:
 sorrows, failures, hopes, plans, joys, sadness, pain!
How many things each one of you,
brothers and sisters, brings to your Sunday Mass!
And the Eternal Priest gathers them in his hands
and by means of the human priest who celebrates
lifts them up to the Father
as the product of the people's labor.
United to my sacrifice present on this altar,
the people are made godlike
and now leave the cathedral
 to keep on working,
 to keep on struggling,
 to keep on suffering,
but ever united with the Eternal Priest,
who remains present in the eucharist
so that we can meet him the next Sunday also.

MAY 28, 1978

Let's not meditate on a word that is disincarnated from reality.

It's very easy to preach a gospel that's the same here in El Salvador as it would be in Guatemala, or in Africa.

Of course, it's the same gospel, just as it's the same sun that brightens the whole world. But just as the sunlight turns into flowers or fruits, according to the needs of the nature that receives it, so God's word has to be incarnated in reality.

And that is what is difficult about the church's preaching. Preaching the gospel without getting involved with reality doesn't bring on any problems, and it's very easy to fulfill the preacher's mission that way.

But to cast the gospel's universal light on our own Salvadoran miseries – and also on our Salvadoran joys and successes – that's what is most beautiful about God's word. That way we know Christ is talking to us, to the community of our archdiocese gathered here to meditate on his divine word.

JUNE 4, 1978

The Well-Being We All Need [45]

The slogan we see all around us these days, "Well-being for All," would be a brilliant formula for expressing "the common good," if the two terms *well-being* and *all* were genuine and sincere. *Well-being* in the sense of *common good* was defined as follows by Vatican Council II:

> The common good comprehends the sum of those conditions of social life by which persons, families, and associations can achieve their fulfillment more fully and more readily.[46]

The fruit of genuine social well-being must not be limited to the aspects of economic production. If genuine well-being is synonymous with the true common good that originates and authorizes a political community, then it has a moral goal, and to achieve this goal it must combine tasks and objectives that are more than merely material. The Council expresses it thus:

> The concrete ways in which the political community organizes its basic structure and constitutes public authority can vary according to the character and historical development of different peoples. But they should always serve to form persons who are educated, peaceable, and kind to all, for the benefit of the whole human family.[47]

This should also be the understanding of the universal purpose expressed in the slogan referred to above, in order for it to be a slogan about the genuine common good. All of us Salvadorans have the right to expect of those who lead our political community that they use the tools of our democracy not just to obtain material advantages of power or money, even though these may be sought "for all," we must also achieve a genuine humanization of all. For human beings are of worth not so much for what they have as for what they are, as Paul VI teaches in the encyclical, "The Development of Peoples."

I have never held that an agrarian or any other type of economic transformation would be adequate by merely distributing property or seeing that the country's wealth reaches all. That is necessary and urgent, but not enough. Well-being must also reach all by putting into practice the constitutional principle of the social function of private property, understood within a sound and intelligent distributive justice. But I say that distributive justice is not enough if it only contemplates material well-being.

There is something of more value than bread and material advantage. There is a sense of innate honor and virtue that the mere possession of material property does not promote. Property is harmful in both its extremes: when it is possessed in excessive abundance or when it is lacking in the case of excessive poverty.

Genuine well-being for all will be the true common good in which genuine channels of true democracy are opened, so that, without fear of repression, all without exception can contribute their bit toward enabling all Salvadorans to fulfill in themselves that model of "persons who are educated, peaceable, and kind to all, for the benefit of the whole human family."

JUNE 6, 1978

Denouncing idolatry has always been a mission
    of the prophets and of the church.
It's no longer the god Baal,

but there are other dreadful gods in our time:
    the god of money,
    the god of power,
    the god of luxury,
    the god of lust.
So many gods enthroned among us!
Hosea's voice could say to today's Christians:
    Don't mix those idolatries
      with the worship of the true God!
    You can't serve two lords,
      the true God and money.
    You can follow only one.[48]

JUNE 11, 1978

Abraham was living quietly in Ur of Chaldea when the Lord told him, "Leave your kindred and go to the land I will show you," without telling him where.[49] Abraham left, walking like a man in a dream, hoping the Lord would tell him where he was to go. Years and generations passed, until at last Abraham's descendants returned from Egypt to the promised land.

God has eternity before him. Only God has security. It is for us to follow humbly wherever God wants to lead, and blessed are those who stay faithful to the ways God inspires them to go and who do not, in order to please others, live with an uneasy conscience in the place where others believe security is to be found.

Leave your kindred, cast off your false security, be converted to the Lord. That is the road without end of our faith's pilgrimage.

JUNE 11, 1978

No one finds it harder
   to tell the evils of his own people than I,
who have the pastoral duty –
   by mandate of the gospel and of Jesus Christ,
who takes away the world's sins –
   of saying what is sin and what must not prevail,
by what ways to walk:
   conversion, faith, mercy.
That is what I have always preached.
Only unworthy and vile slander
   can find anything else in my words.
The word of Hosea, the word of Paul,
   the word of Christ, the word of the church
is what I want to echo,
   to proclaim to my dear people,
to all without exception,
   to sinners as well.
For when Christ corrected those of his time,
   he did not hate them.
He loved them,
   because he wanted to snatch them
from the claws of idolatry, of false positions,
   that they might seek the true way
   where they can find the mercy God offers.
He wanted to forgive them and make them just.

JUNE 11, 1978

There in Rome, the information I gave, the lengthy and calm
dialogs I had with the representatives of the church's central authority, the clarifications I made of certain misunderstandings

or of understandings based on false or biased reports, and my very presence there seemed so providential to me that I give thanks to God that they now know there how I love and support the See of the successor of Peter. They could not doubt my faithfulness to the pope, and I have once more affirmed that, God willing, I will die faithful to Peter's successor, the Vicar of Christ.

I told them: it's easy to preach his teachings theoretically. To follow faithfully the pope's *magisterium* in theory is very easy. But when you try to live those saving teachings, try to incarnate them, try to make them reality in the history of a suffering people like ours – that is when conflicts arise.

Not that I have been unfaithful – never! I think that today I am more faithful than ever, because I experience the trial, the suffering – and the intimate joy – of proclaiming with more than words and lip service a teaching that I have always believed and loved. I am trying to give it life in this community, which the Lord has entrusted to me.

Dear friends, if we are really Catholics, followers of an authentic gospel – and therefore a difficult gospel – if we really want to live up to the name of followers of Christ, let us not be afraid to transform into flesh and blood, into living history, this teaching, which from the pages of the gospel becomes present reality in the teaching of the councils and of the popes, who try to live like true shepherds through the vicissitudes of their times.

JULY 2, 1978

It must have been a moment – I was going to say, of disappointment – when Christ saw the great crowds that followed him, but among them only simple people – peasants, fisherfolk. If perchance any learned persons drew near, he would see them withdraw with disdain, as though laughing at the teaching of that mad preacher.

And when Christ was left alone, raising his eyes to his Father he uttered the fondness, the sorrow, the affliction of his heart: Why, Father, when I have offered them a teaching so sublime, some refuse to accept it from me and others, the simple, do accept it from me? "I give you thanks, Father, for you have hidden these things from the learned and proud, and have revealed them to simple people. Yes, Father, thus you have willed."[50]

The initiative is God's. Jesus Christ is not at fault, nor is the church or the preacher. And when some would sneer that only simple people follow us, here in the gospel is the explanation.

JULY 9, 1978

When Paul VI talked about having to renew the church, and that this was the goal of the Second Vatican Council, he explained very well that renewal does not mean accommodating to the modern ways of the world, which at times are unchristian. Renewal means making the church consistent with the seed that was planted. A tree, however much it grows, remains consistent with its seed. What is important to understand is that God's word is a seed, and it cannot be altered. We would like a teaching more accommodated to our interests. We'd like a preaching that isn't so bothersome, that doesn't cause conflicts.

But when Christ planted the seed, he had conflicts. That seed is the word of the Just One, of the Holy One, of the one who knows what he wanted when he created humanity and nature; and so it guides us, but it collides with sin. It clashes with those who don't want the seed to grow.

JULY 16, 1978

How different it is to preach here, at this moment, than to speak as friends with any one of you!

At this moment, I know that I am being an instrument of the Spirit of God in his church to guide the people, and I can say like Christ: "The Spirit of the Lord is upon me; he has sent me to bring good news to the poor."[51]

The same Spirit that gave life to Christ and gave force to his body born of the Virgin, so that it could be the sacrificial victim for the world's salvation, is the very Spirit that also gives power and inspiration to my throat, to my tongue, to my feeble limbs.

And the same Spirit gives you, God's people, the ability to hear God's word as it should be heard.

I know that many do not hear me with this supernatural Spirit. Of them I can say, as in the parable, it is seed that falls on the highway and the evil one will take it away.[52]

But I know that many do listen to me, as in the parable today, like earth that receives the seed, and the Spirit of God gives that earth, which is your hearts, the ability to hear supernaturally, the grace to be able to listen.

So, as I told you, the preacher not only teaches, but learns. You teach me. Your attention is also for me the Holy Spirit's inspiration. Your rejection would be for me God's rejection also.

That is why I told you the people have a sense of infallibility, called the sense of faith. The Holy Spirit gives it to the humblest woman of the people, to everyone, so that when you listen to a bishop or a priest you can discern. You can at least suspect, "That teaching mustn't be from the gospel."

But when I see such attention, such faith, and especially such conversion, people seeking the church, seeking God, then I say with joy: the finger of God is here.

J U L Y   1 6 ,   1 9 7 8

Evangelizing is not just saying words.
Preaching is relatively easy,
but to live out what is preached –
    as I told the Holy Father in Rome,
to respect the teachings of the Holy See,
    of the *magisterium*,
to praise them, extol them, defend them theoretically
is very easy;
but when one tries to incarnate that teaching
and give it life in a diocese, in a community,
and point out concrete events
that are against that teaching,
    then the conflicts arise.
And this is the life of our archdiocese, dear friends,
because not all are willing
to live a commitment to witness;
not all suffer persecution,
and it is easy to say there is no persecution.
But every priest, religious, or lay person
who wants to announce Christ's gospel in truth
    must suffer persecution.
The witness of life is necessary.
Here I make an appeal that all your lives and mine
be in truth a silent preaching.
Thus is the gospel lived,
    not just by preaching pretty sermons
    and not living them.

JULY 16, 1978

St. Paul speaks of the glorification
that we'll one day be given,
superior to all the pains and sufferings
that can be felt on this earth.
The other day I heard these words of St. Paul
translated to the suffering of a tortured man
who was kept three days with his fingers bound.
As he suffered he said,
"The hope I have and the glory I await
are greater than this suffering."[53]

   Take heart, you that are persecuted.

   Take heart, you that are tortured.

   Take heart, all those who hope for a better land
   and see no horizon.
Your suffering is the condition of the redemption
that was gained only by Christ nailed to a cross.
But afterward came the resurrection.
In Christ's heart the certainty never died
that the world would be redeemed
despite his apparent failure.
We Christians do not fail,
for we bear the Spirit that raised up Christ.

JULY 16, 1978

The first reading speaks of a God who is Providence, a God
who cares for all, a God who governs us.[54]

   How beautiful to know that we are governed by God, under
God's sovereignty! That is what the Holy Bible means when it
says there is no jurisdiction that does not come from God and
authority must be obeyed because it comes from God.

   But it is also saying that the sovereign, the one who com-
mands, may not command except what God wills and that, if an

authority must be respected, it is because it reflects God's sacred dominion.

When human authority becomes abusive of God's law, of right, of liberty, of human dignity, then it is time to cry out like St. Peter, also in the Bible, "We must obey God rather than men."[55]

All authority comes from God, and therefore a ruler may not use it capriciously, but only according to the Lord's will. God's providence wants to govern peoples, and rulers are his ministers, servants of God like all his creatures.

JULY 23, 1978

A merciful God, today's reading calls him.
 Your sovereignty over all makes you pardon all.
 You govern us all with great indulgence
  because you can do all that you want to do.

It would seem to be the other way around.
 Just because you can do all that you want to do,
  you could trample us,
  you could walk over us,
  you could torture us,
  you could treat us cruelly.

But no. Just because you can do what you want to do,
  you love us —
 because you have the resources to be merciful
  and to hope that people will return
  to the right way.
How different from the justice of human beings!

When humans acquire power, how they trample others!
 What tortures, what horrors!
"You can do whatever you want,

and so you are treating me this way."
How many must have spoken thus
    in those horrid dungeons
that shame our civilization:
    those of the police,
    of the *Guardia Nacional,*
wherever there has been torture –
    by the powerful,
    by those who have weapons,
    by those who wear boots to kick with,
        because they can do whatever they want.

But only God can do whatever he wants,
    and this God governs us with kindness.

In a weak person, power becomes cruelty;
    a sense of inferiority
        is carried to the level of brutishness.

    God has no sense of inferiority.
    God is sovereign.
    God can do all,
        and so he judges even his felons,
        even his sinners,
with kindness and mercy.

But this just and merciful God also sanctions,
    because his mercy is not weakness.

JULY 23, 1978

The parable of the wheat and the weeds should lead us,
    brothers and sisters,
to understand the mystery of iniquity,

which is also operative in the church.[56]
The church is not just the wheat crop.
   Bishops, priests, nuns, lay people,
   families, youths, Catholic schools –
should they not all be holy?
Indeed they should.
   Are they?
Sadly, we must say no.
Then the church is false?
   No.
If a church wants to pride itself on having only holy members,
it won't be the true church,
for Christ has said that his church is like a field
where wheat and weeds bear fruit.
While we live in this pilgrim church,
   we have to be together,
   wheat and weeds.

JULY 23, 1978

God has sown goodness.
No child is born evil.
We are all called to holiness.
The values that God has sown in the human heart
and that present-day people esteem so highly
are not rare gems;
   they are things that appear continually.

Why then is there so much evil?
Because the evil inclinations of the human heart
have corrupted people, and they need purification.

The original, pristine human vocation is goodness.
We have all been born for goodness:

no one is born with inclinations to kidnap,
no one is born with inclinations to be a criminal,
no one is born to be a torturer,
no one is born to be a murderer.
We have all been born to be good,
to love one another,
to understand one another.

Why then, Lord, have so many weeds
grown up in your field?
The enemy has done it, says Christ.
People have let weeds grow in their hearts:
evil company,
evil propensities,
evil habits.

Beloved young people,
about to choose your life's vocation,
ponder how we are all called to goodness
and how the older generation –
my own, I regret –
is leaving you a heritage of so much selfishness,
of so much evil.
Renew,
new wheat, newly sown crops,
fields still fresh from God's hand,
children, youths:
be a better world.

JULY 23, 1978

CHAPTER FOUR

Don't Pull Them Up

In those mysterious dungeons
where so many of our brothers and sisters have vanished,
   how many must know terrible secrets,
   how many have hands stained with blood,
   marked by outrages – how many weeds in the harvest!
God waits for them.
Don't pull them up, says Christ – wait.
We wait.
I would like to say, as a brother,
to all those friends whose consciences are uneasy
because they have sinned against God and neighbor:
   You cannot be happy that way;
   the God of love is calling you.
   He wants to forgive you,
   he wants to save you.

JULY 23, 1978

If we really want to reveal the new creation
that God has made within us,
giving us his Spirit

and making us sharers of his divine pleasure,
    let us be led by his Spirit to pray.

St. Paul today tells us:
    The Spirit within you teaches you to ask and to pray
    according to God's desire.
    And the God who discerns spirits
    knows what God's Spirit is asking within your hearts.[57]

How wondrous
that God should start an intimate dialog with humans
by raising them to God's level
and speaking their own language!

And to raise them to God's level,
he has given them his Spirit.

To pray is to converse with God.
Vatican Council II uses a very helpful comparison
saying that God has given humans
the intimate sanctuary of their consciousness
    so that they can enter that private space
    and there speak alone with God
    to decide their own destiny.
We all have a church within ourselves,
    our own consciousness.
There God is,
    God's Spirit.
Blessed are those who do not forsake
that shrine by failing to pray.
Blessed are those who enter often

to speak alone with their God.
   Try it yourselves, brothers and sisters.

Though you feel yourselves sinners,
   tainted,
enter all the more and say:
   Lord,
   correct me,
   I have sinned,
   I have offended you.

Or when you feel the joy of a good act:
   Lord, I give you thanks
   because my conscience is joyful
   and you commend me.

Or when in affliction
you find no one to offer a word of guidance,
   enter your intimate sanctuary,
   and God will show you the way.

Or when you are sad,
like those many mothers
of persons arrested and not seen again,
enter alone with God and say:
   Lord,
   you know where they are.
   You know how they are being treated.

Speak with him.

How beautiful is prayer, my friends,
when it is truly made with God's Spirit inside us
and sharing in God's life!

JULY 23, 1978

Patronal Feasts [58]

In a dizzying race to secularize, many have lost the religious and ecclesial meaning of the patronal feasts of the diocese or of the country. It would be naive to try to stop that race or to lament the loss of traditions that yesterday had their reason for being but today must yield to new needs. What must not be lost, however, is what is essential in the content and in the purpose of the patronal feasts.

The essential thing that our liturgical and popular feasts ought to offer to the diocese and to the nation is a threefold sense – of unity, of transcendence, and of protection. This is what is unchangeable and what should mark the human, moral, and Christian result of our observances, whatever the external garb of the celebration.

The patron is first of all a force for unity, unity in love and in ideal. It is wonderful, the expression of joy and friendship that unites hearts for the patron's holy day. As the universal community, the church forms a wonderful unity amid diversity. But the patron imprints spiritual features on local communities to distinguish them from one another within the harmony of universal unity. Alongside the patron, naturally, stands the hierarchical power of the bishop. He must not ignore the unitive power and character of the patron of the diocese in devising pastoral action suitable to his people's character.

The patron also is a proclamation of transcendence. Amid the church's temporal concerns, the patron is a Christian reminder of its eschatological destiny. But this is not disincarnate eschatology or disincarnate transcendence. As a voice and message from beyond history, the patron is a reminder that what is beyond is fashioned in the here and now of one's own duties. The patron was generally a pilgrim on this earth and, as patron, keeps on accompanying, from eternity, all the ups and downs of God's kingdom, which makes its home and finds its way in history and in the world.

Finally, the feast of the patron awakens a sense of hope and security, because it signifies a power of protection. The patron already enjoys the security of victory by possessing a life fully supported by the Almighty's love. The patron's security and life extend to the protected, and without giving up their own personal efforts they become more enterprising and firm in the struggles of God's kingdom to achieve a happier world for humans.

JULY 28, 1978

It moves one's heart to think:
    Nine months before I was born
    there was a woman who loved me deeply.
She did not know what I was going to be like,
    but she loved me
    because she carried me in her womb.
And when she gave me birth,
    she took me in her arms
    because her love was not just beginning –
    she conceived it along with me.

A mother loves –
and that is why abortion is so abhorrent:
A mother who aborts

is unfaithful to the love that she should have
　　(like God in eternity)
before her child is born.

God is the exquisite likeness
of a mother with child.
God bore me in his womb
　　and loved me and destined me
　　and already thought of my days
　　and of my death.
What will happen to me doesn't matter to me;
God already knows it.

Let us not be afraid, brothers and sisters.
　　We are living through difficult and uncertain days.
　　We do not know if this very evening
　　we will be prisoners
　　or murder victims.
We do not know
　　what the forces of evil will do with us.
But one thing I do know:
　　even those who have disappeared after arrest,
　　even those who are mourned in the mystery of an abduction,
are known and loved by God.
If God allows these disappearances
it is not because he is helpless.
He loves us,
　　he keeps on loving.

He loves our history too, and he knows
where the ways of our land's redemption will lead.
We do not lose hope in this great truth.
This is the true treasure of God's reign:

hope, faith, prayer,
   the intimate force that joins one to God.
Let us pray for this.

JULY 30, 1978

I am glad to see this people,
   come from all the community of the archdiocese
      and from beyond,
   come to inundate its hope,
   its faith,
in the light of Christ.
It seems St. Peter has written for us Salvadorans
that superb second letter
from which is taken today's word of exhortation
   that we keep faithful to the teaching given us,
   based on the power and the glory of Christ
   and on the living witness of the apostles,
who saw with their own eyes the Redeemer's transfiguration,
a witness that confirms the witness of the prophets.
There is found all the Old Testament in Moses and Elijah
and all the New Testament in Peter, James, and John
   confronting the clever fables,
   the teachings of human beings,
   the false redemptions that humans promise,
so that they can trust in him.
And, says St. Peter, almost poetically,
this faith,
   like a lamp burning in the night,
will light up the darkness until the morning star arises.

   It is the night of our history,
   it is the journey of our time,
   it is these difficult hours,

such as our land is undergoing,
    which seem like a night without escape –
until the sun of the transfiguration
brings daylight and hope to the Christian people,
    enlightening our way.
Let us be faithful to it.

Dear brothers and sisters,
    the church knows it is God's lamp,
    light taken from the glowing face of Christ
to enlighten human lives, the lives of peoples,
    the complications and problems
that humans create in their history.
The church feels obliged to speak, to enlighten
    like the lamp in the night.
The church feels compelled to light up the darkness.[59]

AUGUST 6, 1978

The church is a lamp that has to give light, and therefore it must involve itself in tangible reality and thus be able to enlighten the pilgrims who walk on this earth. This concern of the church does not mean that it leaves its own sphere but that it perseveres in its difficult duty of shedding light on concrete affairs.

Out of this concern, the church defends the right of association, and it promotes a vigorous activity of raising consciousness and of organizing among the poor in order to bring about peace and justice. The church, from its commitment to the gospel, supports the just objectives that the organizations likewise seek, and it also points out the injustices and the instances of violence that the people's organizations may commit. Therefore, the church cannot be identified with any organization, even with those that call themselves and feel themselves Christian. The church is not the organization, and the organization is not the church.

If both faith and political vocation have grown in a Christian, concerns of faith cannot be simply identified with a specific political concern. Still less can the church and the organization be identified. And no one can say that only within a certain organization can the Christian demands of the faith be developed. Not every Christian has a political vocation, and political activism is not the only activity that implies a concern for justice. There are also other ways to translate one's faith into work for justice and for the common good.

One cannot insist that the church or its ecclesial symbols become instruments of political activity. To be a good political activist one need not be a Christian, but Christians involved in political activity have an obligation to profess their faith in Christ and to use methods that are congruent with their faith. If a conflict arises in this area between loyalty to the faith and loyalty to the organization, genuine Christians must choose faith and demonstrate that their struggle for justice is for the justice of God's kingdom and no other.

Priests and lay people called to work together with the hierarchy may naturally feel more sympathy for one party or organization than for another, working as they do in a type of evangelization incarnated in the country's tangible reality. But if they realize that the efficacy of the church's mission depends on their being faithful to their own identity, the first goal of their pastoral work will be to be animators and guides in faith and in justice. They will leave the specific tasks that arise from ordinary political action to those who are more expert in evaluating and managing them.

AUGUST 6, 1978

To those who bear in their hand,
or in their consciences,
   the burden of bloodshed,
   of outrages,
   of the victimized, innocent or guilty,
but still victimized in their human dignity,
I say:
   Be converted.
You cannot find God
on those paths of torture and outrages.
God is found on the ways of justice,
   of conversion,
   of truth.

And to those who have received
the awesome charge of governing,
in the name of Christ I recall how urgent
are just laws and solutions for the majority,
who have vital problems
   of livelihood,
   of land,
   of wages.
The good of all, the common good,
has to be an impetus for you,
as charity is for a Christian.

Be mindful of the right to participate that all aspire to,
for everyone can contribute something
to the nation's common good.
Now more than ever a strong authority is needed,
not to seek a mechanical or despotic unity,
   but rather as a moral force
   based on freedom
   and on the responsibility of all,
so that all forces can come together

in spite of their different viewpoints
and even of their opposition to the nation's good.
Give the people opportunity to organize,
   repeal the unjust laws,
   grant amnesty to those who have broken laws
     that are not for the common good,
   stop intimidating the people,
     in particular the rural population.
Set free or arraign in court
   those who have disappeared after arrest
   or are jailed unjustly.
Give those who have been expelled
   or kept from returning for political reasons
the chance to return to the country.

AUGUST 6, 1978

The Council calls creation and its conservation
   a lasting witness to him, to God.[60]

When one looks at creation,
when one sees the maintenance of nature,
so balanced and so wonderful,
and even when one feels the shaking of earthquakes
   or the flames of conflagrations
   or the power of hurricanes –
creation's beauty and the majesty of the phenomena
   that humans can only admire but not control,
like the very storm that Peter knew on the Lake of Gennesaret:
how tiny seem human beings
   before these manifestations in his creation
   of the Creator's omnipotence.
They are witnesses of him, lasting witnesses.
Wherever we open our eyes

or our ears catch the murmur of creation,
God is speaking to us.

AUGUST 13, 1978

There is a more exquisite manifestation of God
that the Council calls supernatural revelation:
    God willed to reveal himself
    and manifest the mystery of his will.
Through Christ and with him through his Spirit
humans can attain to the Father
    and share in the nature of God.
He speaks with humans as friends speak among themselves.
Anyone who has a friend
    understands this beautiful comparison.
There are no secrets,
    there is trust,
    there is unburdening;
    secrets are shared
        without fear of being informed on.
Thus God speaks his secrets,
    his designs for creation,
    for human beings,
    for his church,
what God wants of humanity,
he, the Lord of history.
How beautiful to feel like Adam in paradise,
    where the Bible says God came down
    to converse with him!

These are the delightful moments
that Christ the Son of Man felt.
In the scene that today's gospel reveals to us

he went up the mountain alone to pray.
We often find Christ in dialog with his Father;
he wanted to teach us
    that we must live in continuous converse with him
    and that we must live by his life,
    not live by sin, by lies –
    that we must lose ourselves in the beauty,
    in the sublimity of God,
    giving him thanks for favors received,
    begging pardon for our infidelities,
    praying to him when the limitations of our power
    clash with the greatness asked of us.
We must learn to understand that we have such a capacity
and that God desires to fill up that capacity.

This is the beauty of prayer and of Christian life:
coming to understand that a God
who converses with humans
    has created them
    and has lifted them up,
    with the capacity of saying
    "I" and "you."
What would we give to have such power
    as to create a friend to our taste
    and with a breath of our own life
    to make that friend able to understand us
        and be understood by us
        and converse intimately –
    to know our friend as truly another self?
That is what God has done;
human beings are God's other self.
He has lifted us up
so that he can talk with us and share his joys,

his generosity,
his grandeur.
He is the God who converses with us.

How can we humans live without praying?
How can a person spend
a whole life without thinking of God,
leave empty that capacity for the divine
and never fill it?
Brothers and sisters,
if only my homily today could achieve this:
to awaken an interest in finding
what perhaps one has never found!

AUGUST 13, 1978

"Call no one teacher on earth," said Christ.[61]
My, how rebellious!
But it is the holy rebellion
of one who has found the only one
who must be called Lord.
When one has found that Lord and Teacher
who illumines the truth
in the intimacy of one's own consciousness,
one is truly free.

AUGUST 13, 1978

This dynamic church must enlighten,
but first it *is*.
Philosophy says one must be before one can act.
Before all else, the church has this task:
to be, to build itself up.
I continuously invite you, dear friends,

to view this purpose above all in my poor words.
They do not try to confront anyone;
    I am not fighting with anyone.
    I am helping Christ to build his church
and calling on all of you who are baptized,
who are the church,
    to make yourselves aware,
    to work together,
so that we may make of this pilgrim people
    truly a torch to enlighten the world.
So, let no one hear my words with a polemic spirit.
I don't want to be an opposition,
    as was said of me this week.
I want to be simply an affirmation.
When one says yes to one's own conviction,
    one is not confronting,
    one is simply affirming oneself.
Naturally, some others don't think the same way
and thus confrontation arises,
but not because one means to seek it.

AUGUST 20, 1978

Let me explain what my office is and how I am fulfilling it. I study the word of God to be read on Sunday. I look around me, at my people. I use this word to shed light on my surroundings, and I make a synthesis so as to be able to convey the word to the people and make them light of the world, a people who allow themselves to be guided by principles and not by the earth's idolatries.

Naturally, the idols and idolatries of the earth are irritated by this word, and they would like very much to remove it, to silence it, to kill it. Let happen what God wills, but his word, as

St. Paul said, is not tied down. There will be prophets, whether
priests or lay people – there already are, in abundance – who
understand what God wants to do through his word for our
people.

AUGUST 20, 1978

It is true that the church seeks ideals of peace,
   but it discerns different kinds of violence.
In my pastoral letter I recall how, on the peak of Tabor
   next to Christ transfigured
the five men who appear –
   Moses, Elijah, Peter, James, and John –
are men of violent character,
and they committed terribly violent acts.
Moses killed an Egyptian;
Elijah put to the sword
   the prophets who did not adore the true God;
Peter drew his sword against Malchus
   to defend Christ;
James and John begged Christ to rain fire
   on a town that would not give him lodging.
But I say there what Medellín says:[62]
Christians are peacemakers,
not because they cannot fight,
but because they prefer the force of peace.
And so I invite you,
let us place all that energy
   that God has given our Salvadoran people,
like a torrent,
not at the service of bloodshed, of violence.
We have nothing to fear
   when Salvadorans put all that aggressiveness
   that God has given them

at the service of building true justice,
   of building the order of things
   that truly ought to be defended.

AUGUST 27, 1978

When Pope Paul VI modified the meaning of penance
   for the Christian people,
he said that there are different ways to understand
   the meaning of penance in the Christian life.
Fasting is done in one way in developed countries,
   where people eat well,
and another way in underdeveloped countries,
   where life is almost always lived in a fast.
In this situation, he said, penance means
   to put austerity where there is much well-being
and to put courage and solidarity with the suffering
   and efforts for a better world
     where life is almost a perpetual fast.
This is penance, this is God's will.

SEPTEMBER 3, 1978

St. Paul says in his letter to the Romans
   that a Christian's life, a Christian's body,
   must be presented to God as a living sacrifice
   pleasing to God.[63]
Here, you see, the Bible gives our bodies, our lives,
   a meaning of sacrifice,
   of holocaust,
   a divine meaning that is proper to every person,
   even the lowliest.

I would like everyone to hear this message
who is listening to me,

including those out there listening by radio,
in whatever circumstances they are –
  perhaps a sick person desperate with pain,
  perhaps a poor person who can't find work
    and lacks even food to eat,
  perhaps someone who works and works with no result,
  perhaps another who has too much,
    who has too many comforts and is selfish –
  I don't know who is listening,
but I am grateful for the wonderful attention
  that this packed cathedral is giving me.
I tell you, brothers and sisters in the faith,
that if we offer all this to God –
  suffering, poverty, work, duty, whatever it is –
in order to please God,
  to do his will,
we are being agreeable sacrifices,
  offerings of pleasant aroma on the Father's altar.

SEPTEMBER 3, 1978

The purpose of our life is God's glory.
However lowly a life is,
that is what makes it great.

SEPTEMBER 3, 1978

The church tells every person and every organization
  that pursues a noble or just purpose:
"That's fine, but it's not enough;
incorporate it into Christian redemption.
Unless you liberate yourself from sin,

whose bonds Christ came to burst,
unless you better yourself
 to the point of becoming a child of God
  by grace and holiness,
if your liberation dispenses with Christ
and trusts only in ideologies of the earth,
your liberation is not complete.
I want to serve you,
 leading you by the hand
  toward the true redemption,
  toward your true destiny,
  toward your integral human calling."
This is the church's grand service.

SEPTEMBER 10, 1978

Those who have listened to me here in church on Sundays
 with sincerity,
 without prejudices,
 without hatred,
 without ill will,
 without intending to defend indefensible interests,
those who have listened to me here cannot say
I am giving political or subversive sermons.
All that is simply slander.
You are listening to me at this moment,
and I am saying what I have always said.
What I want to say here in the cathedral pulpit
 is what the church is,
and in the name of the church
 I want to support what is good,

applaud it,
encourage it,
console the victims of atrocities, of injustices,
and also with courage
disclose the atrocities,
the tortures,
the disappearances of prisoners,
the social injustice.
This is not engaging in politics;
this is building up the church
and carrying out the church's duty
as imposed by the church's identity.
My conscience is undisturbed,
and I call on all of you:
Let us build up the true church!

SEPTEMBER 10, 1978

Authority in the church is not command,
but service.
Among Christians,
those who do not become simple as children
cannot enter the kingdom of heaven.
To my shame, as a pastor,
I beg forgiveness from you, my community,
that I have not been able to carry out
as your servant
my role of bishop.
I am not a master,
I am not a boss,
I am not an authority that imposes itself.
I want to be God's servant and yours.

SEPTEMBER 10, 1978

The prophetic mission is a duty of God's people.
So, when I am told in a somewhat mocking tone
    that I think I am a prophet,
I reply: "God be praised! You ought to be one too."
For every Christian,
    all God's people,
    every family,
must develop a prophetic awareness,
convey an awareness of God's mission in the world,
bring it a divine presence
    that makes demands and rejections.

SEPTEMBER 10, 1978

A prophetic people,
as today's gospel says,
    seeks out those who are wrong
so as to win them for God,[64]
and the prophet who speaks
    of the punishment due the negligent sentinel
    also praises the mercy of the God who calls.[65]
Therefore, dear brothers and sisters,
    especially those of you who hate me,
you dear brothers and sisters
    who think I am preaching violence,
    who defame me and know it isn't true,
you that have hands stained
    with murder,
    with torture,
    with atrocity,
    with injustice –

be converted.
I love you deeply.
I am sorry for you
  because you go on the way to ruin.

SEPTEMBER 10, 1978

What says Christ himself?
"Where two or three gather in my name, there am I in their
  midst."[66]
Thank you, Lord.
For where there is a community
that begins to reflect on your words with religious sincerity,
there are you, Christ, the Blessed One, humanity's Liberator.
How my heart is filled with hope by a church
where grassroots communities flourish!
I must ask my dear brother priests
to make communities flourish everywhere –
  in neighborhoods, in villages, among families.
For "where two or three gather in my name,"
  there is the sacramental sign.

SEPTEMBER 10, 1978

Many would like the poor to keep on saying that it is God's will
for them to live that way.

But it is not God's will for some to have everything and others
to have nothing. That cannot be of God. God's will is that all
his children be happy.

SEPTEMBER 10, 1978

"Whoever fulfills the duty of love fulfills the whole law,"
says St. Paul.
   "You shall not steal,
   you shall not kill,
   you shall do no wrong to another –
all this is contained in one phrase:
   you shall love your neighbor."[67]

If there were love of neighbor
there would be no terrorism,
   no repression,
   no selfishness,
   none of such cruel inequalities in society,
   no abductions,
   no crimes.

Love sums up the law.
Not only that, it gives Christian meaning
   to all human relations.
Even those who call themselves atheists,
   when they are humane,
fulfill the essence of the relationship
that God wants among human beings:
Love.

Love gives plenitude to all human duties,
   and without love justice is only the sword.
With love, justice becomes a brother's embrace.
Without love, laws are arduous, repressive, cruel,
   mere policemen.
But when there is love –

security forces would be superfluous;
there would be no jails or tortures,
no will to beat anyone.

SEPTEMBER 10, 1978

What is God's way of thinking?
It is higher than our thoughts,
and – blessed be God –
God does not identify with human thinking.
Many indeed would like, as the song says,
    a pocket-God,
    a God to get along with their idols,
    a God satisfied with the way they pay their workers,
    a God who approves of their atrocities.
How can people pray the Our Father to that God
when they treat him as one of their servants
or one of their employees?

SEPTEMBER 24, 1978

God is kind.
No one can pass judgment on his undertakings.
Appeal to his mercy,
beg, like the good thief, just a remembrance,
and God will give more than a remembrance.

I am trying to show you the God of the Bible,
    the God we have read about today.[68]
Thus is our God –
blessed may he be –
    who has given us to know how he calls at every moment

and at every moment is ready to receive us,
no matter the crimes we have committed.
And so, brothers and sisters,
I repeat again what I have said here so often,
addressing by radio those who perhaps have caused
   so many injustices and acts of violence,
   those who have brought tears to so many homes,
   those who have stained themselves
     with the blood of so many murders,
   those who have hands soiled with tortures,
   those who have calloused their consciences,
who are unmoved
to see under their boots a person abased,
   suffering, perhaps ready to die.
To all of them I say:
   No matter your crimes.
   They are ugly and horrible,
   and you have abased the highest dignity
     of a human person,
but God calls you and forgives you.
And here perhaps arises the aversion of those
   who feel they are laborers from the first hour.
How can I be in heaven with those criminals?
Brothers and sisters,
   in heaven there are no criminals.
The greatest criminal, once he has repented of his sins,
   is now a child of God.

SEPTEMBER 24, 1978

Even the chains of the prison make him joyful,
    says St. Paul,
because "I am making Christ known here
to all the praetorian guardsmen."[69]
It's as though someone were to say,
    "Here in the quarters of the *Guardia*,
        shackled,
    I am making known this Christ in whom I believe
        to whoever wants to listen."
Many praetorians were converted,
for God calls everyone.
God is calling even the torturer.

SEPTEMBER 24, 1978

If at this moment, dear brothers and sisters,
Christians in El Salvador do not feel the crisis
    that is in each Christian's heart,
then they have not reflected on the meaning
    of God's message
    and of his harvest in the world.

Many have already weathered the crisis
    and have committed themselves to God's kingdom.
Many have weathered it in the opposite sense:
    they have settled down in their advantages
    and found it easier to say,
"The church is communist. Why follow it?"

But some indeed are in crisis;
    they do not know what to do.
The blame is not God's or the church's.
Each one's free conscience must decide with whom to stand.
God our Lord is offering wonderful harvests

to those who allow this vine to be planted,
marvelous yield, the fruit of eternal life.
This is God's plan.
The church is the vineyard
    where God's kingdom is ever in crisis.
Blessed are those who feel and live the crisis
and who settle it with a commitment to our Lord.

I am very glad that just at this moment of crisis
many who were asleep have awakened
    and at least ask themselves
    where the truth is to be found.
Look for it.
St. Paul shows us the way:
    with prayer,
    with reflection,
appreciating what is good.
These are wonderful criteria.
Wherever there is "what is noble,
    what is good,
    what is right,"
there is God.[70]
If, besides these natural good things,
there is found grace,
    holiness,
    sacraments,
    the joy of a conscience divinized by God,
there is God.

OCTOBER 8, 1978

CHAPTER FIVE

Evangelizer of the People

Someone used a very flattering comparison in telling me, "Your Sunday homilies are like a university course." I have never intended anything like that, but only to be an ordinary catechist, an evangelizer of the people, nothing else.

But certainly, more important than all the chairs of all the sciences of the human race is the simple chair of evangelization, which teaches people the true meaning of life, their genuine relationship with God, their responsibilities in society. This is what we have tried to do.

OCTOBER 15, 1978

"Here on this mountain I will tear off the veil
    that enshrouds all peoples,
    the cloth that covers all nations.
Here the Lord will annihilate death forever.
Here God will wipe away the tears on every face,
    and his people's shame will depart from all the land."[71]

Let us sing a song of hope
and be filled with cheerful spirit,
knowing that this Christian life,
    which came to us with Christ through the Virgin Mary
    and takes on flesh in all believers,

is the presence of God, who makes us a promise:
No, brothers and sisters,
El Salvador need not always live like this.
"I will tear off the veil of shame
　　that covers it among all peoples.
I will wipe away the tears"
　　of all those mothers who no longer have tears
　　for having wept so much
　　over their children who are not found.
Here too will he take away the sorrow
of all those homes that this Sunday suffer
　　the mystery of dear ones abducted
　　or suffer murder
　　or torture
　　or torment.
That is not of God.
God's banquet will come;
wait for the Lord's hour.
Let us have faith;
all this will pass away
　　like a national nightmare,
and we shall awake to the Lord's great feast.
Let us be filled with this hope.

OCTOBER 15, 1978

Our religion is life.
This is a beautiful truth
　　that I want to remind you of.
I want to recall it to you with gratitude to God,
because the preaching of religion as life
　　is what has given resurrection and life
　　to many who were dead in faith.
It is worthwhile to believe,

it is worthwhile to come to Mass on a Sunday
and nourish oneself there on words of life,
not because so-and-so says them,
but because they are of Christ,
the living one beyond comparison.

Courage, dear friends.
I know that for many the hour of testing has come,
and they have fled as cowards;
catechists, celebrants of the word,
people who shared with us the joys of our meetings,
   have been frightened.
People we thought very strong are frightened away
because they have forgotten
   that this is a religion of life
   and, as life, it must clash
      with the life that is not God's life
    but exists as the kingdom of darkness
      and of sin in the world.

OCTOBER 29, 1978

A Christian community is evangelized
   in order to evangelize.
A light is lit
   in order to give light.
A candle is not lit to be put under a bushel,
   said Christ.
It is lit and put up high
   in order to give light.
That is what a true community is like.
A community is a group of men and women
   who have found the truth in Christ and in his gospel,
   and who follow the truth

and join together to follow it more strongly.
It is not just an individual conversion,
but a community conversion.
It is a family that believes,
a group that accepts God.
In the group, each one finds that the brother or sister
    is a source of strength
and that in moments of weakness they help one another
and, by loving one another and believing,
    they give light and example.
The preacher no longer needs to preach,
for there are Christians who preach by their own lives.
I said once and I repeat today
that if, unhappily, some day they silence our radio
and don't let us write our newspaper,
each of you who believe
    must become a microphone,
    a radio station,
    a loudspeaker,
not to talk, but to call for faith.
I am not afraid that our faith may depend
    only on the archbishop's preaching;
I don't think I'm that important.
I believe that this message,
    which is only a humble echo of God's word,
enters your hearts,
    not because it is mine,
    but because it comes from God.

OCTOBER 29, 1978

I give thanks to God
because you are receiving my word
   as what it truly is, God's word.
For many receive it as a man's word,
   an enemy's word,
   a subversive's word,
   as the word of a man who only desires evil.
That is the sad lot of one who preaches God's word,
to be, like Christ, a sign of contradiction.

But, blessed be God,
all that also means that the vehicle,
even though it be crude and useless,
   is only a vehicle.
What matters is what is in the vehicle:
God's word,
   which is accepted in the hearts
   and which converts,
bringing about holiness and life.
And so, there is much holiness in our communities.

I give thanks to God, and I invite all
   to draw near with me to the eucharist,
which means to give thanks to God,
because there is found the source,
   Christ,
who is the Word made flesh,
   nourishment,
   sacrament,
   life.
Christ it is who now nourishes us,
and from our Sunday eucharist
the word that is preached

becomes a church of sinners
and also a church of holiness.

NOVEMBER 5, 1978

They Both Deny God [72]

"The word *atheism* is applied to very diverse phenomena," says
Vatican Council II.[73] It then goes on to describe a lengthy series
of spiritual attitudes toward religion: "Some expressly deny
God, others declare that nothing can be said about God," and it
mentions pseudoscientific or sociological atheisms and then the
practical atheism of those who "so exalt humanity that faith in
God becomes hollow, though they seem more inclined to affirm
humanity than to deny God." This type of atheism logically in-
cludes the systematic rejection of the transcendental values that
nourish the Christians' hope. The Council describes it thus:

> It holds that religion, by its very nature, is an obstacle to hu-
> man economic and social liberation, since in pointing the hu-
> man spirit toward an illusory future life it deters people from
> the building of the earthly city. Hence, when the defenders of
> this doctrine gain power over the state, they vehemently at-
> tack religion and spread atheism through the means that pub-
> lic authority has at its disposal, especially in the education of
> the young.[74]

The church knows this all too well, both in theory and from experience. It is therefore absurd to say that the church has become Marxist. Since Marxist materialism destroys the church's
transcendent meaning, a Marxist church would be not only self-
destructive but senseless.

But there is an "atheism" that is closer at hand and more dangerous to our church. It is the atheism of capitalism, in which

material possessions are set up as idols and take God's place. Vatican II is the one that points it out:

> Atheism arises at times…from wrongly making certain human goods into absolutes, so that they are then substitutes for God. Present-day civilization, not in itself, but because it is too much wrapped up in earthly affairs, can often make it harder to approach God.[75]

Here, in a capitalism that idolizes money and "human goods," is a danger for us as serious as the other, and perhaps more than the other, which gets the blame for all evils. Which is more serious: to deny God out of a false idea of human liberation, or to deny him out of selfishness raised to the level of idolatry? Who are the greater hypocrites: those who believe in this world to the point of denying openly what is transcendent, or those who use what is transcendent and religious as a tool and justification for their idolatry of the earth?

Both are atheism. Neither is the truth that the church of the gospel teaches so beautifully: "The sublimest reason for human dignity is human beings' call to communion with God."[76]

NOVEMBER 15, 1978

Everyone who struggles for justice,
everyone who makes just claims in unjust surroundings
is working for God's reign,
  even though not a Christian.
The church does not comprise all of God's reign;
God's reign goes beyond the church's boundaries.

The church values everything that is in tune
  with its struggle to set up God's reign.
A church that tries only to keep itself

pure and uncontaminated
would not be a church of God's service to people.
The authentic church is one that does not mind
conversing with prostitutes and publicans and sinners,
    as Christ did –
and with Marxists and those of various political movements –
in order to bring them salvation's true message.

DECEMBER 3, 1978

Some want to keep a gospel so disembodied
    that it doesn't get involved at all
       in the world it must save.
Christ is now in history.
Christ is in the womb of the people.
Christ is now bringing about
    the new heavens and the new earth.

DECEMBER 3, 1978

Christ became a man of his people and of his time:
    He lived as a Jew,
    he worked as a laborer of Nazareth,
    and since then he continues to become incarnate
       in everyone.
If many have distanced themselves from the church,
    it is precisely because the church has somewhat
       estranged itself from humanity.
But a church that can feel as its own all that is human
    and wants to incarnate the pain,
    the hope,
    the affliction of all who suffer and feel joy,

such a church will be Christ loved and awaited,
   Christ present.
And that depends on us.

DECEMBER 3, 1978

When we speak of the church of the poor,
we are not using Marxist dialectic,
as though there were another church of the rich.
What we are saying is that Christ,
inspired by the Spirit of God,
declared, "The Lord has sent me
to preach good news to the poor" –
   words of the Bible –
so that to hear him one must become poor.[77]

DECEMBER 3, 1978

The Christian knows that Christ has been working
   in humanity for twenty centuries
and that the person that is converted to Christ
   is the new human being that society needs
     to organize a world
according to God's heart.

DECEMBER 3, 1978

Advent should admonish us to discover
in each brother or sister that we greet,
in each friend whose hand we shake,
in each beggar who asks for bread,
in each worker who wants to use the right to join a union,

in each peasant who looks for work in the coffee groves,
the face of Christ.
Then it would not be possible to rob them,
to cheat them,
to deny them their rights.
They are Christ,
and whatever is done to them
Christ will take as done to himself.
This is what Advent is:
Christ living among us.

DECEMBER 3, 1978

The person who feels the emptiness of hunger for God
is the opposite of the self-sufficient person.
In this sense, *rich* means the proud,
rich means even the poor who have no property
but who think they need nothing, not even God.
This is the wealth that is abominable in God's eyes,
what the humble but forceful Virgin speaks of:
"He sent away empty-handed the rich" –
those who think they have everything –
"and filled with good things the hungry" –
those who have need of God.[78]

DECEMBER 3, 1978

Advent is not just four weeks preparing for Christmas.
Advent is the church's life.
Advent is Christ's presence
as he uses his preachers,
his priests,
his catechists,
his Catholic schools,

all the effort
   meant to bring about God's true reign,
telling humanity that Isaiah's prophecy is now fulfilled:
   Emmanuel – God with us.

DECEMBER 3, 1978

God comes, and his ways are near to us.
God saves in history.
Each person's life, each one's history,
   is the meeting place God comes to.
How satisfying to know one need not go to the desert
   to meet him,
need not go to some particular spot in the world.
God is in your own heart.[79]

DECEMBER 10, 1978

Who will put a prophet's eloquence into my words
to shake from their inertia
all those who kneel before the riches of the earth –
who would like gold, money, lands, power, political life
   to be their everlasting gods?
All that is going to end.
There will remain only the satisfaction of having been,
   in regard to money or political life,
   a person faithful to God's will.
One must learn to manage the relative and transitory
   things of earth according to his will,
   not make them absolutes.
There is only one absolute: he who awaits us
   in the heaven that will not pass away.

DECEMBER 10, 1978

Let's Preserve Christmas[80]

In celebrating Christmas, many Christians today are doing exactly the opposite of what Christians did in the past. By celebrating Christmas, ancient Christianity managed to christianize the pagan feast of the sun. Today's Christians' neopaganism is managing to paganize Christmas.

Jesus was not born on December 25 exactly. The Christian liturgy chose that date in order to give a Christian meaning to the Roman feast of the unvanquished sun. The pagans of the Roman Empire celebrated the sun's rebirth during the longest night of the year. That midnight was considered as the starting point of the sun's march, which then began to overcome the darkness. It was easy for the Christians to substitute Jesus Christ for the sun and to make the birth of Christ, Sun of Justice, coincide liturgically with the pagan celebration of the birth of the sun. The centuries that followed have proved the church's genius, for bit by bit the meaning of Christmas pushed into oblivion the jovial pagan celebration and filled the entire world with the joy of the Redeemer's birth. Today even unbelievers sense that something divine entered history during that night without compare. We all feel that the child born that night is a child of our family, and that the brightness of God's glory that the angels carol makes of that night the loveliest day, a day when God himself offers us his peace and invites us to be men and women of good will.

What a shame that all of that Christian inspiration with which our liturgy christened a pagan festival has been betrayed by many Christians, who today surrender that spiritual conquest to paganism. To make the values of commerce and of

worldly gaiety prevail over the gospel meaning of Christmas is
nothing short of a cowardly surrender on the part of Christians.

A return to the spirituality of a genuine Christmas will be a
noble gesture of solidarity with Christianity's spiritual victories
in the world. A celebration of Christ's birth with a sense of adoration, love, and gratitude toward the God who loved us even to
the folly of giving us his own Son, will be to arrange our life so
that the peace that only God can give may brighten it like a sun.

DECEMBER 15, 1978

I invite you this week, in this hour
    when El Salvador seems to have no place for joy,
to listen to St. Paul repeat to us:
    "Be always joyful.
    Be constant in prayer.
    In every circumstance give thanks.
    This is God's will for you in Christ Jesus."[81]
The Christian, the Christian community, must not despair.
If someone dies in the family,
    we must not weep like people without hope.
If the skies have darkened in our nation's history,
    let us not lose hope.
We are a community of hope,
and like the Israelites in Babylon,
    let us hope for the hour of liberation.
It will come.
    It will come because God is faithful, says St. Paul.
This joy must be like a prayer.
"He who called you is faithful,"
    and he will keep his promises.[82]

DECEMBER 17, 1978

I know that God's Spirit, who made Christ's body in Mary's womb and keeps making the church in history here in the archdiocese, is a Spirit that is hovering – in the words of Genesis – over a new creation.

I sense that there is something new in the archdiocese.

I am a man, frail and limited, and I do not know what is happening, but I do know that God knows.

My role as pastor is what St. Paul tells me today: "Do not quench the Spirit."[83]

If I say in an authoritarian way to a priest: "Don't do that!" or to a community: "Don't go that way!" and try to set myself up as if I were the Holy Spirit and set about making a church to my liking, I would be quenching the Spirit.

But St. Paul also tells me: "Test everything and keep what is good."[84]

I pray very much to the Holy Spirit for that; it is called the gift of discernment.

DECEMBER 17, 1978

If Christ had become incarnate now
   and were a thirty-year-old man today,
he could be here in the cathedral
   and we wouldn't know him from the rest of you –
a thirty-year-old man, a peasant from Nazareth,
   here in the cathedral like any peasant
   from our countryside.
The Son of God made flesh would be here
   and we wouldn't know him –
     one completely like us.

DECEMBER 17, 1978

How shameful to think that perhaps pagans,
   people with no faith in Christ,
may be better than we
   and nearer to God's reign.
Remember how Christ received a pagan centurion
   and told him, "I'll go and cure your servant"?
The centurion, full of humility and confidence,
   said, "No, Lord. I am not worthy that you go there.
Just say a word
   and my servant will be cured."
Christ marveled, says the gospel, and he said,
   "Truly, I have not found such faith in Israel."[85]
I say:
Christ will also say of this church:
outside the limits of Catholicism
perhaps there is more faith,
   more holiness.
So we must not extinguish the Spirit.
The Spirit is not the monopoly of a movement,
   even of a Christian movement,
of a hierarchy, or priesthood, or religious congregation.
The Spirit is free,
and he wants men and women,
wherever they are,
to realize their vocation to find Christ,
   who became flesh to save all human flesh.
Yes, to save all, dear brothers and sisters.
I know that some people come to the cathedral
   who have even lost the faith or are non-Christians.
Let them be welcome.
And if this message is saying something to them,
I ask them to reflect in their inner consciousness,

for, like Christ, I can tell them:
the kingdom of God is not far from you,
    God's kingdom is within your heart.
Seek it, and you will find it.

DECEMBER 17, 1978

The Bible has a very meaningful expression:
    The Spirit makes all things new.[86]
We are those who grow old,
    and we want everyone made to our aged pattern.
The Spirit is never old;
the Spirit is always young.

DECEMBER 17, 1978

God keeps on saving in history.
And so, in turning once again
    to the episode of Christ's birth at Bethlehem,
we come not to recall Christ's birth twenty centuries ago,
but to live that birth here,
in the twentieth century, this year,
in our own Christmas here in El Salvador.
By the light of these Bible readings
we must continue all the history
that God has in his eternal mind,
even to the concrete events
    of our abductions,
    of our tortures,
    of our own sad history.
That is where we are to find our God.

DECEMBER 24, 1978

This is the Christian's joy:
    I know that I am a thought in God,
    no matter how insignificant I may be –
    the most abandoned of beings,
        one no one thinks of.
Today, when we think of Christmas gifts,
    how many outcasts no one thinks of!
Think to yourselves, you that are outcasts,
    you that feel you are nothing in history:
"I know that I am a thought in God."

Would that my voice might reach the imprisoned
    like a ray of light, of Christmas hope –
might say also to you,
    the sick,
    the elderly in the home for the aged,
    the hospital patients,
    you that live in shacks and shantytowns,
    you coffee harvesters trying to garner your only wage
        for the whole year,
    you that are tortured:
God's eternal purpose has thought of all of you.
He loves you,
and, like Mary, he incarnates that thought in his womb.

DECEMBER 24, 1978

The Council says humanity's mystery can be explained
    only in the mystery of the God who became human.[87]
If people want to look into their own mystery –
    the meaning of their pain,
        of their work,
        of their suffering,
        of their hope –

let them put themselves next to Christ.
If they accomplish what Christ accomplished –
  doing the Father's will,
   filling themselves with the life
    that Christ gives the world –
they are fulfilling themselves as true human beings.
If I find, on comparing myself with Christ,
  that my life is a contrast, the opposite of his,
then my life is a disaster.
I cannot explain that mystery
  except by returning to Christ,
who gives authentic features
  to a person who wants to be genuinely human.

DECEMBER 24, 1978

No one can celebrate a genuine Christmas
  without being truly poor.
The self-sufficient,
the proud,
those who, because they have everything,
  look down on others,
those who have no need even of God –
  for them there will be no Christmas.
Only the poor,
the hungry,
those who need someone to come on their behalf,
  will have that someone.
That someone is God,
   Emmanuel,
   God-with-us.
Without poverty of spirit
  there can be no abundance of God.

DECEMBER 24, 1978

When the poor have nowhere to rest their bodies,
 and their children fleeing from the cold
 find only hammocks
  strung up in the fields and coffee groves,
we must recall that the Savior's good news is for all.
The happiness of the Lord who created us
 to fulfill his salvation is everyone's.

DECEMBER 24, 1978

Mary is not an idol.
The only Savior is God, Jesus Christ,
but Mary is the human instrument,
 the daughter of Adam,
 the daughter of Israel,
 a people's embodiment,
 sister of our race,
who by her holiness was able to incarnate in history
 God's divine life.
The true homage that a Christian can make to Mary
 is, like her,
to make the effort to incarnate God's life
 in the fluctuations of our fleeting history.

DECEMBER 24, 1978

Christ put his classroom of redemption
 among the poor –
not because money is evil,
but because money often makes slaves
 of those who worship the things of earth
 and forget about God.

DECEMBER 25, 1978

Along with you, my dear brothers and sisters, I too need to receive the good tidings tonight. As shepherd I must announce it, but as shepherd I must also be one of those shepherds of Bethlehem and receive from the angels the news that stirs our hearts. Let us receive it, you and I, with the same simplicity and humility as those shepherds did. The more simple and humble, the more poor and detached from ourselves, the more full of troubles and problems we are, the more bewildering life's ways, all the more must we look up to the skies and hear the great news: "A Savior is born to you." And let us listen in chorus to that great news, sung throughout the universe: "Glory to God in the heavens, and on earth peace to those whom God loves."[88]

DECEMBER 25, 1978

Through the church's eyes I see the great deficiencies
    in our Christianity
that Medellín has now defined for us:
    superstitions,
    traditionalism,
    scandal taken because of the truth preached
        by the church.
And those who have money even publish those scandals
    as though they were defending genuine values.
They don't realize that they are defending the indefensible:
    a lie, a falsehood, a lifeless traditionalism,
    and, much worse, certain economic interests,
which, lamentably, the church served.
But that was a sin of the church,
deceiving and not telling the truth
    when it should have.[89]

DECEMBER 31, 1978 (FEAST OF THE HOLY FAMILY)

There are families where the faith is not developed,
because what is given is traditions
    poisoned by economic and political interests
    and wrapped up with things of faith.
They want a religion that will merely support
    those interests.
And when the church protests against
    such selfishness, sins, and abuses,
    then it is thought to be departing from the truth,
and these Christians, with their children and all,
    go away and continue to live traditions
    that are not true Christian traditions.

DECEMBER 31, 1978

Simeon says, "He is a sign of contradiction."[90]
The good, and the bad who repent through him,
    will receive mercy and pardon.
But he will also be the ruin of many,
    because the sinfulness,
    the selfishness,
    the pride of many
        will reject him.
Christ is a stumbling block.
And so, those who reject me do me an immense honor,
because I somewhat resemble Jesus Christ,
    who was also a stumbling block.
Simeon prophesied that the church, following Christ,
    would have to be like him.

DECEMBER 31, 1978

I was told this week that I should be careful,
that something was being plotted against my life.
    I trust in the Lord,
    and I know that the ways of providence
    protect one who tries to serve him.

JANUARY 7, 1979

The pastoral and evangelical teaching of Vatican Council II,
which in 1968 became also the pastoral policy for Latin America, proclaimed a total salvation, and it continues to raise questions for us now at the dawn of a new Medellín to take place at
Puebla.[91] This teaching declares that the liberation Christ has
brought is of the whole human being. The whole person must
be saved: body and soul, individual and society. God's reign
must be established now on earth.

    That reign of God finds itself hindered, manacled, by many
idolatrous misuses of money and power. Those false gods must
be overthrown, just as the first evangelizers in the Americas
overthrew the false gods that our natives adored. Today the
idols are different. They are called money, they are called political interests, they are called national security. As idolatries, they
are trying to displace God from his altar. The church declares
that people can be happy only when, like the magi, they adore
the one true God.

JANUARY 7, 1979

With the symbolic gifts of incense, gold, and myrrh,
    the wise men bring the pain, the sorrows,
    and the concerns of their peoples

to beg salvation from the only one who can give it.
So it is in our own history.
Each Sunday when I speak of the specific events of the week,
   I am only a poor adorer of the Lord, telling him:
Lord, I bring you what the people produce,
   what the interaction of these people
      of El Salvador,
   rich and poor, rulers and ruled,
      brings forth.
This is what we bring the Lord.

JANUARY 7, 1979

My position as pastor obliges me to solidarity
   with everyone who suffers
and to embody
   every effort for human freedom and dignity.

JANUARY 7, 1979

Christ says his reign is not of this world.

As Pope Pius XI explained when he decreed the feast of Christ the King, that does not mean that Christ is isolated from the power and wealth of earth.

It means that he will use a different basis, a religious basis, to judge the consciences of political leaders and of the rich (and of the poor also), judging them from the eschatological and transcendent perspective of God's reign.

JANUARY 14, 1979

CHAPTER SIX

God's Justice

Peoples are free to choose the political system they want
  but not free to do whatever they feel like.
  They will have to be judged by God's justice
  in the political or social system they choose.
God is the judge of all social systems.
Neither the gospel nor the church can be monopolized
  by any political or social movement.

JANUARY 14, 1979

The present form of the world passes away,
and there remains only the joy of having used this world
  to establish God's rule here.
All pomp, all triumphs, all selfish capitalism,
  all the false successes of life will pass
  with the world's form.
All of that passes away.
What does not pass away is love.
When one has turned money, property, work in one's calling
  into service of others,
then the joy of sharing
  and the feeling that all are one's family
does not pass away.
In the evening of life you will be judged on love.[92]

JANUARY 21, 1979

I wish to affirm that my preaching is not political.
It naturally touches on the political –
and it touches the people's real lives –
but it does so in order to illuminate those realities
and to tell people what it is that God wants
and what it is that he does not want.

JANUARY 21, 1979

No one can serve two lords.
There is only one God,
and that God will either be the true one,
    who asks us to give things up when they become sin,
or it will be the god of money,
    who makes us turn our back on Christianity's God.

JANUARY 21, 1979

The psychotic campaign against Christian communities –
    isn't that persecution?
Isn't the trampling of the people's human rights
    also persecution?
The church considers this its ministry:
    to defend God's image in human beings.

JANUARY 21, 1979

One can perfectly well be a nuncio or a military chaplain, provided one is converted to the gospel.[93] If these duties are carried
out with a genuine sense of being a church that tries first of all
to be faithful to the gospel rather than to earthly advantages –
rather than to the advantages of a diplomatic or military ca-
reer – then indeed there can and should be representatives in

the midst of the diplomatic and the military worlds. But they must be truly the voices of the gospel and of the church. That is where the problem seems to be: conversion to the gospel.[94]

FEBRUARY 9, 1979

In our preaching to rich and poor, it is not that we pander to the sins of the poor and ignore the virtues of the rich. Both have sins and both need conversion. But the poor, in their condition of need, are disposed to conversion. They are more conscious of their need of God.

All of us, if we really want to know the meaning of conversion and of faith and confidence in another, must become poor, or at least make the cause of the poor our own inner motivation. That is when one begins to experience faith and conversion: when one has the heart of the poor, when one knows that financial capital, political influence, and power are worthless, and that without God we are nothing.

To feel that need of God is faith and conversion.[95]

FEBRUARY 18, 1979

To try to preach without referring to the history
    one preaches in is not to preach the gospel.
Many would like a preaching so spiritualized
    that it leaves sinners unbothered
and does not term idolaters
    those who kneel before money and power.
A preaching that says nothing
    about the sinful environment
in which the gospel is reflected upon
    is not the gospel.

FEBRUARY 18, 1979

There are lots of fawners, lots of false prophets, and – in times of conflict like ours – lots of pens for hire and words for sale. But that is not truth.

I heard that when they got my bag from customs two days ago, someone said, "There goes the truth." That remark fills me with confidence, because in my bag I haven't brought contraband or lies. I bring the truth. I went to Puebla to learn more of the truth.

When a journalist asked me, "They say that after Puebla you will change your preaching. What do you think?" I told him, "The truth doesn't have to change. The truth will still be said, perhaps more precisely, but always within our limitations. It's the particular word of a man who has his own style and way of being, but who is only God's instrument in the history of events."

FEBRUARY 18, 1979

I cannot change
    except to seek to follow the gospel more closely.
And I can quite simply call to everyone:
    let us be converted
    so that Christ may look upon our faith
    and have mercy on us.

FEBRUARY 18, 1979

Like the prophets' words
    proclaiming to Babylon's captives
    times of joy and freedom,
the church's word
    calling to love, reconciliation, and pardon
    can seem like a mockery

when others hold to violence, kidnapping, and terrorism.
But the church will never walk that path,
    and whatever is said to that effect is false.
It is a slander that only enhances in the church
    the glory of our persecution.

FEBRUARY 18, 1979

To build the unity and authenticity of the church,
    the true bride of Christ,
is the joy of the pastor who wishes for Christ
    all love, all homage, and all solidarity.
If in any way my poor human presence blurs his image,
    then I say like John the Baptist:
I must disappear, but he, the church's bridegroom,
    must grow.
I must bear no rivalry toward him
    but simply serve him with humility and love
and rejoice that he wins the heart of his church.

FEBRUARY 25, 1979

I recognize my limitations and my miseries,
but I cannot renounce the role that Christ has given me:
    to be the sign
    of the church's unity, teaching, and truth
        in the archdiocese.

FEBRUARY 25, 1979

I don't want to be an anti,
    against anybody.
I simply want to be the builder of a great affirmation:

the affirmation of God,
  who loves us
  and who wants to save us.

The church renews itself. We cannot preserve old traditions
that no longer have any reason for being, much less those structures in which sin has enthroned itself and from which come
abuses, injustices, and disorders.

  We cannot call a society, a government, or a situation Christian when our brothers and sisters suffer so much in those invet-
erate and unjust structures.

FEBRUARY 25, 1979

When we speak of the church of the poor,
  we are simply telling also the rich:
Turn your eyes to this church
  and concern yourselves for the poor
    as for yourselves.
At Puebla we said the poor are a concern of Christ,
  who will say at the end of life,
"Whatever you did to one of these poor ones,
  you did to me."[96]

MARCH 4, 1979

If we are worth anything,
  it is not because we have more money
    or more talent
    or more human qualities.
Insofar as we are worth anything,

it is because we are grafted onto Christ's life,
    his cross and resurrection.
That is a person's measure.

MARCH 4, 1979

You know that the air and water are being polluted, as is everything we touch and live with, and we go on corrupting the nature that we need. We don't realize we have a commitment to
God to take care of nature. To cut down a tree, to waste water
when there is so much lack of it, to let buses poison our atmosphere with those noxious fumes from their exhausts, to burn
rubbish haphazardly – all that concerns our alliance with God.

MARCH 11, 1979

It would be too bad if the same thing were to happen with the
Puebla document as with Medellín's. Many Catholics, out of
prejudice, at times out of ignorance, did not put it into practice.

If our own archdiocese has become a scene of conflict, let
there be no doubt in your minds, it is because of its desire to be
faithful to this new evangelization.

From Vatican Council II until now, and in particular in the
meetings of Latin American bishops, the demand is for an evangelization that is committed and fearless.

MARCH 11, 1979

A church that suffers no persecution but enjoys the privileges
and support of the things of the earth – beware! – is not the true
church of Jesus Christ.

MARCH 11, 1979

I look at you, dear friends, and I know
that my humble ministry is only that of Moses:
    to transmit the word – "Thus says the Lord."
And what pleasure it gives me when you say
    in your intimate hearts,
    or at times in words or in letters I receive,
what the people replied to Moses:
    "We will do all that Yahweh has ordained."[97]

MARCH 18, 1979

The other day a priest told me that a man wanted to go to con-
fession who hadn't done so for forty years. He said he wanted to
be converted, as he had heard about here in the cathedral.

    When they say I preach political matters, I refer to these testi-
monies of conversion to God. That is what I seek: conversion to
God. If I point to political matters here, it is often because of the
corruption of political affairs, so that those whom God loves
even when they are mired in sin may be converted too.

MARCH 18, 1979

Would that I were being listened to
    by those whose hands are soiled with murders!
They are many, alas.
    For torturers are also murderers;
one who begins to torture does not know
    where it will end.
We have seen torture victims taken to hospitals to die
    under all sorts of deceitful stratagems.
Torturers too are killers, murderers;
    they do not respect the sacredness of life.
No one may raise a hand against another,

because human beings are God's image.
"You shall not kill!"[98]
I also wish to mention the enormous disgrace
    of killing even in the mother's womb.
Abortion, too, is killing, an abhorrent crime.
    And it is even one's mother who abuses and kills!
"You shall not kill!"
When Christ perfected this commandment, he said:
When you begin to hate,
    you have also begun to kill.[99]

MARCH 18, 1979

I am not a politician or sociologist or economist.
I am not the one responsible for solving
    the country's political and economic problems.
There are others, lay people,
    who have that tremendous responsibility.
From my post as pastor, I only call upon them
    to use those talents that God has given them.
As pastor I have the task –
    and this is what I try to do –
of building the true church of our Lord, Jesus Christ.

MARCH 25, 1979

Those who, in the biblical phrase, would save their lives – that is, those who want to get along, who don't want commitments, who don't want to get into problems, who want to stay outside of a situation that demands the involvement of all of us – they will lose their lives.

What a terrible thing to have lived quite comfortably, with no suffering, not getting involved in problems, quite tranquil, quite settled, with good connections politically, economically, so-cially – lacking nothing, having everything.

To what good?

They will lose their lives.

"But those who for love of me uproot themselves and accom-pany the people and go with the poor in their suffering and become incarnated and feel as their own the pain and the abuse – they will secure their lives, because my Father will re-ward them."

Brothers and sisters, God's word calls us to this today. Let me tell you with all the conviction I can muster, it is worthwhile to be a Christian.[100]

APRIL 1, 1979

To each one of us Christ is saying:

If you want your life and mission to be fruitful
   like mine, do as I.

Be converted into a seed that lets itself be buried.
   Let yourself be killed.

Do not be afraid.

Those who shun suffering will remain alone.
   No one is more alone than the selfish.

But if you give your life out of love for others,
   as I give mine for all,

you will reap a great harvest.

You will have the deepest satisfactions.

Do not fear death or threats;
   the Lord goes with you.

APRIL 1, 1979

At this moment, in the name of all my priests,
  I beg pardon
for not having shown all the fortitude the gospel asks
  in serving the people that we must lead,
for having confused them at times,
  softening too much the message of the cross,
which is hard.

APRIL 1, 1979

The message of Holy Week has perhaps greater meaning for the present time than for any time before. Amid so many voices and cries from oppressed and oppressors, amid so much machinery of repression and so many moans of victims, amid the selfishness of those who refuse to hear the protest of the hungry, in the presence of rightful efforts made for social justice, and in particular as we live surrounded by a virtual environment of terrorism, vengeance, and violence – what good it would do us all to raise our problems and our feelings and personal or group efforts to the transcendent level that Christ calls us to from his cross in Holy Week: to God's justice and his merciful love.[101]

APRIL 6, 1979

The church cannot agree with the forces that put their hope only in violence.

The church does not want the liberation it preaches to be confused with liberations that are only political and temporal.

The church does concern itself with earthly liberation – it feels pain for those who suffer, for the illiterate, for those without electricity, without a roof, without a home.

But it knows that human misfortune is found not only there. It is inside, deeper, in the heart – in sin.

While supporting all the people's just claims, the church wants to lift those demands to a higher plane and free people from the chains that are sin, death, and hell.

It wants to tell us to work to be truly free, with a freedom that begins in the heart: the freedom of God's children – the freedom that makes us into God's children by taking from us the chains of sin.

APRIL 8, 1979

If my person is repulsive to some,
    who would therefore silence my voice,
let them not look at me,
    but at him who bids me tell them: Love one another!
It is not me they hear,
    but the Lord, who is love
and wants to make us his own
    by the sign of his love. [102]

APRIL 12, 1979

A civilization of love
    that did not demand justice of people
would not be a true civilization:
    it would not delineate genuine human relations.
It is a caricature of love to try to cover over
    with alms what is lacking in justice,
to patch over with an appearance of benevolence
    when social justice is missing.
True love begins by demanding what is just
    in the relations of those who love.

APRIL 12, 1979

If there is not truth in love, there is hypocrisy. Often, fine words are said, handshakes given, perhaps even a kiss, but at bottom there is no truth.

A civilization where trust of one to another is lost, where there is so much lying and no truth, has no foundation of love. There can't be love where there is falsehood.

Our environment lacks truth. And when the truth is spoken, it gives offense, and the voices that speak the truth are put to silence.

APRIL 12, 1979

God is not failing us when we don't feel his presence.

Let's not say: God doesn't do what I pray for so much, and therefore I don't pray anymore.

God exists, and he exists even more, the farther you feel from him.

God is closer to you when you think he is farther away and doesn't hear you.

When you feel the anguished desire for God to come near because you don't feel him present, then God is very close to your anguish.

When are we going to understand that God not only gives happiness but also tests our faithfulness in moments of affliction?

It is then that prayer and religion have most merit: when one is faithful in spite of not feeling the Lord's presence.

Let us learn from that cry of Christ that God is always our Father and never forsakes us, and that we are closer to him than we think.

APRIL 13, 1979 (GOOD FRIDAY)

You that have so much social sensitivity, you that cannot stand this unjust situation in our land: fine – God has given you that sensitivity, and if you have a call to political activism, God be blessed. Develop it.

But look: don't waste that call; don't waste that political and social sensitivity on earthly hatred, vengeance, and violence.

Lift up your hearts. Look at the things above.[103]

APRIL 15, 1979 (EASTER SUNDAY)

"Receive the Holy Spirit."
Christ himself explains:
    "As my Father sent me, I send you."
He means that the church is born
    with this breath of his,
and the mission that the church will bear to the world
    for all time will be that of Christ dead and risen.
The church celebrates its liturgy and preaches its message
    only for this:
    to save from sin,
    to save from slaveries,
    to overthrow idolatries,
    to proclaim the one God, who loves us.
That will be the church's difficult mission,
and it knows that in fulfilling that mission,
    which earned for Christ a cross and humiliations,
it will have to be ready also not to betray that message
and, if necessary, to suffer martyrdom like him –
suffer the cross, humiliation, persecution.[104]

APRIL 22, 1979

You have to understand clearly that the conflict is between the government and the people. There is conflict with the church because we take the people's side. I insist that the church is not looking for a fight with the government, and for my part I do not want disputes with the government. When they tell me I am a subversive and that I meddle in political matters, I say it's not true. I try to define the church's mission, which is a prolongation of Christ's. The church must save the people and be with them in their search for justice. Also, it must not let them follow ways of hatred, vengeance, or unjust violence. In this sense, we accompany the people, a people that suffers greatly. Of course, those that trample the people must be in conflict with the church.[105]

JUNE 2, 1979

It is wrong to be sad.
Christians cannot be pessimists.
Christians must always nourish in their hearts
    the fullness of joy.
Try it, brothers and sisters;
I have tried it many times and in the darkest moments,
when slander and persecution were at their worst:
    to unite myself intimately with Christ, my friend,
    and to feel a comfort
    that all the joys of the earth do not give –
the joy of feeling oneself close to God,
even when humans do not understand one.
It is the deepest joy the heart can have.

MAY 20, 1979

Sincerely, I have never favored anyone,
    because I have been committed only to my God.
I have always proclaimed my autonomy
    so as to be able to praise what is good in anyone

as well as to be able to rebuke with total freedom
     what is evil and unjust in anyone.
That is what the church is here for.
The political circumstances of peoples change,
     and the church cannot be a toy of varying conditions.
The church must always be the horizon of God's love,
     which I have tried to explain this morning.
Christian love surpasses the categories
     of all regimes and systems.
If today it is democracy and tomorrow socialism
     and later something else,
that is not the church's concern.
It is your concern, you who are the people,
     you who have the right to organize
          with the freedom that is every people's.
Organize your social system.
The church will always stay outside, autonomous,
     in order to be, in whatever system,
the conscience and judge of the attitudes
     of those who manage or live in those systems or regimes.

MAY 20, 1979

Transcendence means breaking through encirclements.
It means not letting oneself be imprisoned by matter.
It means saying in one's mind:
     I am above all the things that try to enchain me.
Neither death nor life
     nor money nor power nor flattery —
nothing can take from one this transcendent calling.
There is something beyond history.
There is something that moves the threshold
     of matter and time.
There is something called the transcendent,

the eschatological,
the beyond,
the final goal.
God, who does not let things contain him
  but who contains all,
is the goal to which the risen Christ calls us.

MAY 27, 1979

How many there are that would do better not to call themselves
Christians, because they have no faith.
  They have more faith in their money and possessions than in
the God who fashioned their possessions and their money.

JUNE 3, 1979

It's amusing:
This week I received accusations from both extremes –
from the extreme right, that I am a communist;
from the extreme left, that I am joining the right.
I am not with the right or with the left.
I am trying to be faithful to the word
  that the Lord bids me preach,
    to the message that cannot change,
which tells both sides the good they do
  and the injustices they commit.

JUNE 3, 1979

The church is not an opposition party.
The church is a force of God in the people,
  a force of inspiration
    so that the people may forge their own destiny.
The church does not want to impose

political or social systems.
It must not. That is not its field of competence.
Rather, the church invokes the freedom of peoples
    not to have a single standard imposed on them,
    but for individuals to be allowed to further
        through their skills and technology
    what the people deserves,
    what the people thinks it wants,
as the architect of its own destiny,
free to choose its own way to achieve the destiny
    that God points out to it.

JUNE 10, 1979

He is not a distant God –
    transcendent, yes, infinite,
but a God close at hand here on earth.

JUNE 10, 1979

CHAPTER SEVEN

The Bright Light of Christ

When the priest raises the host and says,
    "Let us proclaim the mystery of faith,"
you reply what you sense within:
    "Christ has died. Christ is risen."
This is the eucharist:
    proclamation of the Lord's death,
    proclamation of his eternal life,
    optimism of men and women who know
that they are following,
even amid the darkness and confusion of our history,
    the bright light of Christ,
        eternal life.

JUNE 17, 1979

The Christian wears the sureness of Christ
    and is the seed of salvation.
If there is hope of a new world,
    of a new nation,
    of a more just order,
    of a reflection of God's kingdom in our society,
brothers and sisters,
    surely you Christians are the ones
    who will bring about this wonder of a new world —

but only when we all are really communicators of the life
that we come to receive in the eucharist at our Sunday Mass,
communicators of the seed that will transform the world.

J U N E 1 7 , 1 9 7 9

The eucharist makes us look back to Calvary twenty centuries
ago and beyond that to Moses and the old covenant, an incom-
parable horizon of history.

But it also looks ahead to the future, to the eternal, eschatological, and definitive horizon that presents itself as a demanding ideal to all political systems, to all social struggles, to
all those concerned for the earth.

The church does not ignore the earth, but in the eucharist it
says to all who work on earth: look beyond. Each time the Victim is lifted up at Mass, Christ's call is heard: "Until we drink it
anew in my Father's kingdom."

And the people reply: "Come, Lord Jesus."

There is a hope. They are a people that march to encounter
the Lord. Death is not the end. Death is the opening of
eternity's portal.

That is why I say: all the blood, all the dead, all the mysteries
of iniquity and sin, all the tortures, all those dungeons of our
security forces, where unfortunately many persons slowly die,
do not mean they are lost forever.

J U N E 1 7 , 1 9 7 9

When individuals or groups want to work only for the earth and
have no horizon of eternity and don't care about religious hori-
zons, they are not complete liberators. You can't trust them. To-

day they struggle for power, and once in power, tomorrow they will be the worst repressors if they have no horizon that goes beyond history to sanction the good and the bad that we do on earth. That way there can be no true justice or effective working for it.

JUNE 17, 1979

When we leave Mass,
we ought to go out
the way Moses descended Mount Sinai:
   with his face shining,
   with his heart brave and strong
     to face the world's difficulties.

JUNE 17, 1979

It makes me sad to think that some people don't evolve. They say, "Everything the church does today is wrong, because it isn't the way we did things as children." They think back to their school days and long for a static Christianity, one that preserves things, like a museum.

Christianity is not like that, and neither is the gospel. It has to be the leaven of the present time. It must point out not the sins of the times of Moses and Egypt nor of the times of Christ and Pilate and Herod and the Roman Empire, but the sins of today, here in El Salvador, the ones you must live among in these historical surroundings. We must be the seed of holiness and unity here amid the dreadful things that are going on among our own people, with whom we are in communion as a church.

JUNE 17, 1979

Let us not put our trust
   in earthly liberation movements.
Yes, they are providential,
but only if they do not forget
that all the liberating force in the world
comes from Christ.

JUNE 24, 1979

Life is always sacred.
The Lord's commandment,
   Thou shalt not kill,
makes all life sacred.
Blood poured out,
   even a sinner's,
always cries out to God.[106]

JUNE 30, 1979

There is a phrase in Puebla's "Message to the Peoples of Latin America" that I think shows the way for those who believe that, when the church proclaims itself the church of the poor, it is biased and scornful of the rich. Not at all. The message is universal. God wants to save the rich also.

But precisely because he wants to save them, he tells them they can't be saved unless they are converted to the Christ who indeed lives among the poor. So Puebla's message says that being poor consists in this: "Accepting and taking up the cause of the poor, as though accepting and taking it up as one's own cause and the cause of Christ himself. 'Whatever you do to one of these brothers or sisters of mine, no matter how humble, you do to me.'"[107]

JULY 1, 1979

We should not feel superior when we help anyone.
Those who give materially receive spiritually.
There is an exchange of property
that is understood only in a true spirit of poverty,
which makes the rich feel they are
close brothers and sisters of the poor,
and makes the poor feel they are equal givers
and not inferior to the rich.
The giving is mutual,
"that there may be equality," as St. Paul says.[108]

JULY 1, 1979

Death is the sign of sin,
and sin produces death right in our midst:
   violence,
   murder,
   torture (which leaves so many dead),
   hacking with machetes,
   throwing into the sea –
   people discarded!
All this is the reign of hell.

JULY 1, 1979

"Most gladly, therefore," says St. Paul humbly,
"will I rather glory in my weaknesses
   that the power of Christ may rest upon me.
Therefore I live content in my weaknesses,
in reproaches, in hardships, in persecution and distress
   for the sake of Christ."
Brothers and sisters,
what a beautiful experience it is

to try to follow Christ a little bit
and for that to receive the broadside of insults,
   of disagreements,
   of slanders,
   of lost friendships,
   of being suspect!
All this was prophesied.[109]

JULY 8, 1979

If some day they take the radio station away from us,
   if they close down our newspaper,
   if they don't let us speak,
   if they kill all the priests and the bishop too,
and you are left, a people without priests,
each one of you must be God's microphone,
each one of you must be a messenger,
a prophet.
The church will always exist
as long as there is one baptized person.
And that one baptized person who is left in the world
is responsible before the world for holding aloft
the banner of the Lord's truth
and of his divine justice.

JULY 8, 1979

Because it is God's work, we don't fear
   the prophetic mission the Lord has entrusted to us.
I can imagine someone saying,
   "So now he thinks he's a prophet!"
No, it's not that I think I'm a prophet;

it's that you and I are a prophetic people.
Everyone baptized has received a share
    in Christ's prophetic mission.

JULY 8, 1979

When Father Rafael Palacios was murdered in Santa Tecla,
    and his body was laid out here,
I said that he was still preaching,
    calling attention
not only to crimes outside the church
    but to sins within the church.
The prophet also decries sins inside the church.
    And why not?
We bishops, popes, priests, nuns, Catholic educators –
    we are human, and as humans we are sinful
and we need someone to be a prophet for us too
    and call us to conversion
and not let us set up religion
    as something untouchable.
Religion needs prophets, and thank God we have them,
    because it would be a sad church
that felt itself owner of the truth
    and rejected everything else.
A church that only condemns,
    a church that sees sin only in others
and does not look at the beam in its own eye,
    is not the authentic church of Christ.

JULY 8, 1979

The church, in its zeal to convert to the gospel, is seeing that its place is by the side of the poor, of the outraged, of the rejected, and that in their name it must speak and demand their rights.

But many persons belonging to the upper classes and feeling as if they owned the church think that the church is abandoning them and slipping away from its spiritual mission: it no longer preaches what is spiritual, it only preaches politics.

It's not that. The church is pointing out sin, and society must listen to that accusation and be converted and so become what God wants.

JULY 8, 1979

Mary, Star of Evangelization [110]

July 16 is an important date on the calendar of popular devotion. It is the feast of Our Lady of Mount Carmel. I recall something very accurate that a missionary said in expressing his admiration for the deep hold that this devotion has among us. He called Our Lady of Mount Carmel "our people's best missionary."

Indeed, I believe there is not a village in El Salvador where the appeal of the Blessed Virgin under the title of Our Lady of Mount Carmel is not felt on this feast day. This is so whether in the general rejoicing of a patronal festival or in a confraternity's simple observance, whether attending Mass or saying a prayer at the altar of Our Lady of Mount Carmel, whether in the village church or in some hamlet or in a home where a family preserves as a precious heirloom an image venerated by their grandparents.

Today, when pastoral experts in their deliberations and briefings are placing great importance on folk religion or popular devotion, the devotion to Our Lady of Mount Carmel is a phenomenon that deserves our attention. We should nurture it as one of those providential resources that the church enjoys for performing its essential task of evangelizing.

In the Magna Carta of evangelization, the exhortation "Evangelization in the Modern World," the late Paul VI used the pastoral experience of the world's bishops to put forth effective norms for ascertaining the exceptional values of these popular devotions. There is no doubt that these enthusiastic religious displays include many deviations, such as fanaticism, superstition, selfish interest, and even doctrinal error, along with the important positive elements of evangelization. But, when properly used, these expressions of our people's soul are genuine worship of our God and, for many, perhaps the only opportunities for a meeting with the Lord.

A pilgrimage to Our Lady of Mount Carmel, or the action of preparing to receive the classic scapular, or of recalling and renewing this alliance with Mary, can lead us to the goal of evangelization, which is sincere conversion and the expression, through the sacraments, of our adherence to the gospel and its hard demands. There should thus be no doubt that July 16 is a privileged day for our pastoral work.

The feast of Our Lady of Mount Carmel is thus a precious heritage of today's church, which is the timeless church. It must do with its inherited treasures what is done with any inheritance – not squander it but manage it well.

It would be unforgivable to destroy or to belittle these lovely and pious expressions of our people merely because they do not fit more sophisticated theological criteria. The wise thing to do is to take these means that our early evangelizers left us and enhance them with the resources of pastoral renewal.

To those whom the Lord has put in charge of church communities, pastoral charity should suggest the norms to follow in regard to popular piety, which is so fruitful and yet at the same time so vulnerable. Above all, one must be sensitive to it, quick to appreciate its inner nature and undeniable values, and ready to help it overcome its risks of deviation. When it is properly guided, this popular piety can increasingly become a genuine encounter with God in Jesus Christ for the masses of our people.[111]

If this is the case for popular piety in general, then the teaching of Paul VI will be even more valid when those masses of people surround the Virgin Mary like loving children. The same document becomingly calls her the Star of Evangelization.

JULY 13, 1979

Remember, I am trying to speak as a member of a people, of a diocese.

Although it is true that I am the bishop of the diocese, still I am not the only one with a prophetic mission.

It is my whole people, all of my priests, all my religious, the Catholic schools, and all who form the Catholic community.

In the name of all of you, beloved lay people who listen to me and reflect with me, I tell what our prophetic mission is, what we must preach with our witnessing and with our words before the Salvadoran people, who so much need this Christian light.

You and I are responsible for seeing that Christ's message reaches everyone.[112]

JULY 15, 1979

I am glad, brothers and sisters,
that our church is persecuted
precisely for its preferential option for the poor
    and for trying to become incarnate
        in the interest of the poor
    and for saying to all the people,

to rulers,
to the rich and powerful:
  unless you become poor,
  unless you have a concern
    for the poverty of our people
    as though they were your own family,
you will not be able to save society.

JULY 15, 1979

What good are beautiful highways and airports,
  beautiful buildings full of spacious apartments,
if they are only put together
with the blood of the poor,
who are not going to enjoy them?

JULY 15, 1979

Christ arisen has put in history's womb
  the beginning of a new world.
To come to Mass on Sunday
  is to immerse oneself in that beginning,
which again becomes present
  and is celebrated on the altar at Mass.
And we who go forth from Mass know
  we have proclaimed the death that saved the world
and proclaimed the resurrection of Christ,
  who lives as hope,
so that all the universe of heaven and earth
  may join together,
all things in heaven and on earth
  may come together in Christ.

JULY 15, 1979

The human race of the twentieth century
   has climbed to the moon,
has uncovered the secret of the atom,
   and what else may it not discover?
The Lord's command is fulfilled:
   Subdue the earth![113]
But the absolute human dominion over the earth
   will be what is proclaimed today:
bringing all things of heaven and earth together
   in Christ.
Then humanity hallowed will put under God's reign
   this world, which is now the slave of sin,
and set it at the feet of Christ,
   and Christ at the feet of God.
This is the bringing together that was God's design
   before the world existed.
And when history comes to its end,
   this will be God's fulfillment:
Christ,
   the sum of all things.
All that history has been,
   all that we do ourselves,
good or bad,
   will be measured by God's design;
and there will remain only those who have labored
   to put things under Christ's rule.
All that has tried to rebel against God's plan in Christ
   is false.
It will not last;
it will be for history's waste heap.

JULY 15, 1979

Jeremiah rebukes the false shepherds, telling them:

Woe to shepherds who scatter the people!
Shepherds who tend my people,
you have scattered my sheep,
driven them out,
not watched over them.
And so I will demand an accounting
of the evil you have done.

Let us ponder this. Beyond the goodness or badness of govern-
ments and shepherds there is a God who prompts the good
shepherd to govern well, who inspires the good actions of those
who cooperate with him, but who is a just God, threatening to
demand a rigorous accounting of evil things done in carrying
out the noble function of government.[114]

JULY 22, 1979

Christ is presented to us as the shepherd king,
    king and shepherd of all the world's peoples,
        of all of history.
He holds the key to history's outcome
    and to the crises of its peoples.
Only if they look to him
    can the peoples find solutions.
If we turn our backs on Christ,
    we will keep on living without meaning,
        like a scattered flock.
But what is truly grand
    is that Christ identifies himself with his people,
        with the baptized of all times,
in order to carry out his regal mission,

his mission of king.
It is for us, hierarchy and people, to proclaim
   the eternal, sole, and universal kingship of Christ
and to bring it about
   that all peoples, families, and persons submit to him.
His is not a despotic regime,
   but a regime of love.
It is the goal of our freedom,
as St. Paul says:
   to be free in order to love in Christ Jesus.[115]

JULY 2 2 , 1 9 7 9

When someone makes power an absolute and an idol and turns
against God's laws, against human rights, violating the people's
rights, then we cannot say that such authority comes from God.

   If it is not lawfully directed as God wills, the people must
obey up to a certain point out of love for the objective common
good, which is the nation's reason for being, but they still retain
the right to seek justice.

JULY 2 2 , 1 9 7 9

Christ has representatives here and now in the world:
   us, his church, the community.
And so, when I focus on the week gone by,
   I attend to a work that is proper for the church.
It should be the principal task
   of us priests, nuns, and faithful –
of all pastoral workers.
   We are not involved in politics;
we turn the gospel's light on the political scene,
   but the main thing for us

is to light the lamp of the gospel
in our communities.[116]

JULY 22, 1979

I want to repeat to you what I said once before:
the shepherd does not want security
while they give no security to his flock.

JULY 22, 1979

Christ invokes eternal justice –
not like on this earth, where even though
you petition the president of the Supreme Court
everything stays the same.
He is not Christ.
But there is a Christ above him,
who will demand an accounting of him
and will demand an accounting of all the accomplices
in this unjust situation in El Salvador.

JULY 29, 1979

These homilies try to be this people's voice.
They try to be the voice of those
who have no voice.
And so, without doubt, they displease those
who have too much voice.

JULY 29, 1979

Let not the church's mission
of evangelizing and working for justice
be confused with subversive activities.

It is very different –
   unless the gospel is to be called subversive
because it does indeed touch the foundations
   of an order that should not exist,
      because it is unjust.

AUGUST 6, 1979

The only violence that the gospel admits
   is violence to oneself.
When Christ lets himself be killed,
   that is violence – letting oneself be killed.
Violence to oneself is more effective than violence to others.
It is very easy to kill,
   especially when one has weapons,
but how hard it is to let oneself be killed
   for love of the people!

AUGUST 12, 1979

I denounce especially the absolutizing of wealth.
This is the great evil in El Salvador:
   wealth, private property,
      as an untouchable absolute.
Woe to the one who touches that high-tension wire!
It burns.

AUGUST 12, 1979

How it delights me in humble villages
when the people and the children come crowding around!
Or you arrive at the town and they come out to meet you.

They come with trust
  because they know
  that you are bringing them God's message.

AUGUST 12, 1979

We had a charming visit yesterday in San Antonio Los Ranchos. Those simple people say they understand well the word that is preached in our homilies.

How absurd is the misunderstanding of those who do not want to hear, the misunderstanding of pride and arrogance.

As Christ said, "I give you thanks, Father, because you have revealed these things to the simple and humble and do not reveal them to the proud and arrogant."[117]

AUGUST 12, 1979

Above all, what I want in my preaching is to place within reach of everyone, even the simplest, the grand message of the gospel, which I serve with all my heart and would not want to be distorted.

I don't want the message that is received to be the chronicle of the week, or criticism of the government, or accusation of sins.

That is something extra; it is like the light of the gospel hitting those concrete events.

The principal thing that I would like you to take away with you from my preaching is the light of the gospel.

With that light you yourselves can illuminate, not the events that I point out, but concrete events of your own, those of your families, those in your lives, among your friends, in your job.

Preaching is done so that all Christians who ponder the gospel can, in enlightening their own lives, illuminate with the principles of Christ the events that surround them.

AUGUST 12, 1979

Arson Cannot Touch Ideas[118]

Every clue indicates that a criminal hand set fire to *La Crónica del Pueblo* last Saturday night. If it was so, we are facing another manifestation of the irrationality that provokes repressive violence against freedom of expression.

When others have a different opinion or, worse, when another points out one's sins, only two rational and humane stances are possible: to dialog in order to persuade the other that one is right, or manfully to admit the wrong one is accused of and with greater courage to turn away from it. In other words, ideas are combated with ideas. To resort to physical force – not to speak of brute force – in order to silence the expression of thought is the sign of reversion to an age of cave dwellers. Persons capable of setting fire to – or, worse yet, capable of ordering the burning of – the shop where a newspaper is printed that publishes ideas not agreeing with theirs and that points out their sins, not only show an inability to dialog, but reveal themselves to be on the lowest rung of cultural development.

We can only repudiate this barbarism and confirm once again the existence of powers that are sustaining unjust structures of sinfulness. At the same time, the burning of the printing plant of *La Crónica del Pueblo* testifies to the glorious risk that anyone runs who dares to publicize, in the people's defense, the outrageous injustices of those powers. The ashes continue to speak out. The voice of truth, the loving service to the people's noble interests, the intelligence and heart of those who raise those banners, have not been burned. The arson should serve only as an incentive to be reborn, like the legendary phoenix from its own ashes.

The people should help that their voice be heard again from the same rostrum, contributing with their moral and financial support so that *La Crónica del Pueblo* may very soon be rebuilt from the ruins.

AUGUST 20, 1979

I have tried to make the church's voice transparent.
Perhaps I am unsuccessful
    because there is much ill will,
    much ignorance,
    and much idolatry,
and idolaters don't want their idol cast aside.
But still this voice wants to affirm once more
that this is what I mean to proclaim:
the Christ,
who says he does not seek the things of earth
    except to save them.
It makes me laugh when they say I am struggling for power.
How could I be a president or a cabinet minister?
God has called me to be a priest,
    to serve through my church
    and through my priesthood.

AUGUST 26, 1979

Yesterday, in San Juan Opico, television channel 13 of Mexico asked me, "If you or the church were offered the leadership of a revolution, would you accept it?" I replied:

It would be an absurdity. The church is not on earth for that. The church is not here to captain an army or to carry on a revolution, but to be the mother of unity. It remains autonomous between two parties that struggle in order to be able to say to each what is just and what is unjust, and when there are sins of warfare to be able to oppose what must not be done even in situations of conflict. The church wants to be always the voice of Christ, the bread that comes down from heaven for the life, for the light, for the salvation of the world.

Beloved fellow workers in the church, I beg you, let us manifest in the most transparent form this thought of Christ, this transcendence of the church that Pope Paul VI spoke of. If the church proclaimed a different liberation, not that of Christ – one that is not liberation from sin, one that will not lead God's children to heaven, to eternal life; if the church mixed itself up with liberations that were only political, social, or economic – then it would lose its original force and would have no right to speak of liberation in God's name.

AUGUST 26, 1979

I want to use this occasion to reply to those
who want to put me at odds with the Holy See.
The archbishop of San Salvador is proud
of being in communion with the Holy Father.
He respects and loves the successor of Peter.
I know that I would not serve you well,
beloved people of God,
if I were to tear you off from the unity of the church.
Far be it from me!
I would rather die a thousand times
than be a schismatic bishop!

AUGUST 26, 1979

What good is it to have beautiful churches of which Christ could say what he says to the Pharisees in today's gospel: "Your worship is in vain"?[119]

That is what happens with much sumptuous worship, with lots of flowers and so forth and invited guests and all that. Where is the adoration in Spirit and in truth?

I think there is a lesson here for us, dear friends. Let me be the first to accept it and to try to interpret it.

Perhaps I have not known how to carry out properly my duty as a priest of God's worship. Perhaps my fellow priests and I have made worship a matter of arranging the altar beautifully and maybe charging higher fees because it was better decorated. We have made a business of it!

Therefore God, as though entering Jerusalem with a whip, tells us, "You have made my house of prayer a den of thieves!"[120] We all have to stop and think. We are all guilty.

SEPTEMBER 2, 1979

There have been some recent labor conflicts that have produced disappointment because of the intransigence of some of the participants. But there has also been some excellent collective bargaining that sets us an example of how we can negotiate matters reasonably.

To be fair, I would like to note that in recent days I have met businessmen who maintain good labor relations with their workers, even beyond what the law requires. They are ready for a new and better climate to be created in the country in every respect. I say we must not reject such views, even though they are very imperfect and tiny lights. They are lights of hope.

We are not demagogically in favor of one social class; we are in favor of God's reign, and we want to prompt to justice, love, and understanding wherever there is a heart well disposed.

El Salvador's liberation need not mean so much bloodshed; there is still time. If we all bring to bear the goodwill to renounce material things and seek those of divine worth, we can certainly find the way. Naturally, there must be the courage to yield in regard to what has become an untouchable institution, one at the base of all forms of violence: institutionalized violence, the country's injustice.

SEPTEMBER 2, 1979

St. James exhorts us to accept with meekness the word
planted in us, which is able to save us.[121]
Only this word is able to save us.

To believe, to hope:
this is the Christian's grace in our time.
When many give up hope,
when it seems to them the nation has nowhere to go,
as though it were all over,
the Christian says: No,
we have not yet begun.
We are still awaiting God's grace.
With certainty, it is just beginning to be built on this earth,
and we will be a blessed nation
and will escape from so much evil.
A time will come when there will be no abductions,
when we'll be happy
and can walk our streets
and our countryside without fear
of being tortured or kidnapped.

That time will come!
We have a song: "I have faith that all will change."
It must change if we truly believe

in the word that saves
and place our trust in it.

For me, this is the greatest honor in the mission
the Lord has entrusted to me:
to be maintaining that hope
and that faith in God's people
and to tell them:
People of God, be worthy of that name.

SEPTEMBER 2, 1979

CHAPTER EIGHT

Option for the Poor

I would not want to live the life of many of today's powerful, who don't live a real life. They live under guard, they live with uneasy consciences, they live in anxiety. That is not life.

If you obey God's law, you will live. Although they kill me, I have no need.[122]

If I die with a good conscience, with a clean heart that has produced only works of goodness – what can death do to me?

Thank God, we have these models, our beloved pastoral workers who shared the dangers of our pastoral work even to the risk of being killed. When I celebrate the eucharist with you, I feel them present. Each priest killed is for me a new concelebrant in the eucharist of our archdiocese. I know that they are here giving us encouragement by having known how to die without fear, because each one's conscience was committed to this law of the Lord: the preferential option for the poor.

SEPTEMBER 2, 1979

If I have the joy of possessing heaven,
I would not mind being in that heaven
near to those who today declare themselves my enemies,
   because there we will not be enemies.
I am never anyone's enemy.
But let those who without cause want to be my enemies

be converted to love,
and in love we shall meet in the blessedness of God.

Those who do not understand transcendence
    cannot understand us.
When we speak of injustice here below
    and denounce it,
they think we are playing politics.
It is in the name of God's just reign
that we denounce the injustices of the earth.

SEPTEMBER 2, 1979

I believe that the bishop always
    has much to learn from his people.
Precisely in those charisms
    that the Spirit gives to the people
the bishop finds the touchstone
    of his humility and of his authenticity.

SEPTEMBER 9, 1979

When we say "for the poor,"
we do not take sides with one social class, please note.
What we do, according to Puebla,
is invite all social classes,
rich and poor without distinction,
saying to everyone:
    Let us take seriously the cause of the poor
    as though it were our own –
indeed, as what it really is, the cause of Jesus Christ,
who on the final judgment day will call to salvation

those who treated the poor with faith in him:
"Whatever you did to one of these poor ones –
the neglected, blind, lame, deaf, mute –
you did to me." [123]

SEPTEMBER 9, 1979

Unfortunately, brothers and sisters, we are the product
of a spiritualized, individualistic education.
We were taught:
    try to save your soul and don't worry about the rest.
We told the suffering:
    be patient, heaven will follow, hang on.
No, that's not right, that's not salvation!
That's not the salvation Christ brought.
The salvation Christ brings
    is a salvation from every bondage
    that oppresses human beings.

SEPTEMBER 9, 1979

The human progress that Christ wants to promote
    is that of whole persons
        in their transcendent dimension
        and their historical dimension,
        in their spiritual dimension
        and their bodily dimension.
Whole persons must be saved,
persons in their social relationships,
    who won't consider some people more human than others,
    but will view all as brothers and sisters
    and give preference to the weakest and neediest.
This is the integral human salvation
    that the church wants to bring about –

a hard mission!
Often the church will be cataloged
    with communistic or revolutionary subversives.
But the church knows what its revolution is:
the revolution of Christ's love.

SEPTEMBER 9, 1979

I believe that today more than ever in El Salvador
    we need to know Christ.
Today needs Christians, and from Christianity
    will come humanity's true liberators.
Otherwise, we'll be given
    violent, aggressive political movements
of the extreme right or the extreme left,
but we won't be given true human beings.
From Christianity, from you,
    beloved brothers and sisters,
communities that ponder God's word
    as we are doing today
in order to know Christ's mystery,
will come the true liberators the nation needs.

Let us be today's Christians.
    Let us not take fright
at the boldness of today's church.
With Christ's light let us illuminate
even the most hideous caverns of the human person:
    torture, jail, plunder, want, chronic illness.
The oppressed must be saved,
    not with a revolutionary salvation,
    in merely human fashion,
but with the holy revolution of the Son of Man,
who dies on the cross to cleanse God's image,

which is soiled in today's humanity,
a humanity so enslaved,
   so selfish, so sinful.

SEPTEMBER 23, 1979

I think the saints have been the most ambitious people,
those who have wanted to be truly great,
and they are the only truly great persons.
Earthly heroisms cannot attain the heights of a saint.
That is my ambition for you and for me:
   to be great,
   ambitiously great,
because we are God's images
and we cannot be content with mediocre greatness.

SEPTEMBER 23, 1979

This hour of trial will pass
and the ideal so many Christians died for
   will survive resplendent.
It is a black night that we are living,
but Christianity discerns that beyond the night
   the dawn already glows.
The hope that does not fail is carried in the heart.
Christ goes with us!

SEPTEMBER 23, 1979

Persecution must be
so that those who bear that deep hope in their souls
   may put it to the test,
so that perhaps the unbelieving may thus be converted
and see that history's horizon does not end with life

but reaches far beyond,
where the ideals of God's true children extend.

SEPTEMBER 23, 1979

When I summon my priests, religious communities, and pastoral workers to our pastoral labor, it is to build our church.

I am asked, "And when tomorrow things have been settled, what will the church do?"

I reply, "It will keep on being the same."

The church is not developing itself for opportunistic purposes. It is trying to be of the present time, at each moment being ever the church. It will feel fortunate if tomorrow in a more just order it need not speak about so many injustices, but it will always have the task of building itself on the foundation of the gospel.

We will have that work to do in peace or persecution.

SEPTEMBER 23, 1979

I will not tire of declaring that if we really want an effective end to violence we must remove the violence that lies at the root of all violence: structural violence, social injustice, exclusion of citizens from the management of the country, repression. All this is what constitutes the primal cause, from which the rest flows naturally.

SEPTEMBER 23, 1979

Anyone who is chosen, for society's need,
   to be a cabinet member,
   to be president of the republic,
   to be archbishop –
   to be a servant –

is the servant of God's people.
That must not be forgotten.
The attitude to be taken in these offices is not
"I'm in charge here! What I want must be done."
You are only a poor servant of God.
You must be at the Lord's beck and call
    to serve the people according to God's will
    and not according to your whim.

SEPTEMBER 23, 1979

With admiration I give thanks to God that so many gifts of the
Spirit are present in you, God's people, religious communities,
grassroots church communities, ordinary people, peasants. If I
were envious, like the persons in the gospel or in today's first
reading, I would say, "Stop them! Don't let them say anything!
Only I, the bishop, can speak."

No, I have to listen to what the Spirit says through his
people. Only then do I receive it from the people and analyze it
and, along with the people, turn it into construction of the
church.

So it is we must build our church, respecting the charism of
the bishop, who discerns and who unifies, who brings into one
the variety of different charisms. And the hierarchy and priests
must respect the grand deposit of faith that the Spirit entrusts to
God's people. What Moses desired, often comes about: "Would
that all the Lord's people were prophets and would receive the
Lord's Spirit!"

I think this is happening in our archdiocese: it's the people
that are receiving God's Spirit. When I visit the communities, I
respect them and I try to give direction to the great spiritual
wealth that I find even in the humblest and simplest of people.

This building in harmony is what the Lord asks of us.[124]

SEPTEMBER 30, 1979

Let us each endeavor to see what are our own charisms
    or those of our group.
When we look around and see other charisms,
    perhaps showier and lovelier than what God has given us,
let us not feel envious like the disciples of Jesus or Moses:
    "Stop them!"
Absolutely not! Instead, let us listen to Jesus:
    "If they prophesy in my name, they can't be against us.
    Let them be."
And Moses says: "Would that all the people
    might feel themselves flooded with the Spirit."
Indeed, his prophecy is fulfilled in our baptism:
    by our baptism we all join the church's great charism.
Among vocations, charisms, and ways of being,
    what huge differences there are!
Some receive the calling of priest,
    another that of religious,
others that of marriage or of single life.
    Some are called to be professionals
and others, laborers;
nothing's wrong with one job or the other.
The point is to be able to bring them to bear
    on the community's welfare.
If God gives you a vocation to political activism
and you organize the people for their common good,
then use that gift of God.
    It too is a vocation.
Political action is a vocation, and not all have it;
you can't get everyone into an organization.
Likewise, I can't push everyone into the priesthood,
and the married can't tell everyone to enter marriage.
All have to find their own vocation.
Let's respect what God says to each man or woman,

but let us also, all of us, contribute
   to the lovely and varied unity
of God's kingdom and of the church.

SEPTEMBER 30, 1979

I call on all of you,
   makers of so many families,
   builders of so many homes:
Let each family in El Salvador not be a hindrance
   to the urgent changes that society needs.
Let no family isolate itself from society as a whole
   because it is itself well off.
No one marries just so the two of them can be happy;
   marriage has a great social function.
It must be the torch that lights up the way
   to new liberations for other marriages around it.
From the home must come the man or woman
   able to promote the changes needed
   in politics, in society, in the ways of justice:
changes that will not come about
   as long as home life opposes them.

But it will be so easy once boys and girls are trained
   in the heart of each family
to aspire
not to have more
   but to be more,
not to grab everything
   but to give abundantly to others.
They must be educated for love.

Loving is what the family is all about,
and loving means giving oneself,

surrendering oneself to the well-being of all
and working for the common happiness.

OCTOBER 7, 1979

The liberation that Christianity preaches is a liberation from
something that enslaves, for something that ennobles us.

Those who talk only about the enslavement, about the nega-
tive part of liberation, do not have all the power that the church
can give one.

It struggles, yes, against the earth's enslavements, against oppression, against misery, against hunger. All that's true – but, for
what? For something.

St. Paul uses a beautiful expression: to be free for love.[125] To
be free for something positive, that is what Christ means when
he says, "Follow me."

OCTOBER 14, 1979

Let us follow Christ, let us believe in him. Let us be sure that
God, that Jesus Christ, has the power to save our people if we,
instead of turning our backs on him – like the young man who
had not the courage to follow him – say to him, like Peter: "We
have left all, Lord."[126]

What can we do for this people? Surely the Lord will inspire
us to know what to do. All classes in El Salvador can do much.
When Puebla calls on the experts to give a special place to wisdom and faith amid their advances in learning, it also makes an
appeal to members of government, to members of the intellec-
tual and university world, to scientists, experts, and shapers of
technological society, to the directors of the mass media, to
artists, jurists, laborers, peasants, businessmen, economists, the
military.

To the military it says:

> We remind you, with Medellín, that "you have the mission of guaranteeing the citizens' political freedoms, rather than obstructing them."[127] Be conscious of your mission: to guarantee the peace and security of all. Never abuse your power. Rather, be the defenders of the power of right and law. Foster a free, participatory, and pluralistic society.[128]

And I conclude with this sentence of Puebla:

> Let all, finally, contribute to the normal working of society. Let professional and business people undertake their mission in a spirit of service to the people, who look to them to defend their lives and their rights and to further their welfare.[129]

OCTOBER 14, 1979

The service the church renders to Salvadorans at this moment is, above all, that of being herself: to be church. She would not be any help if she converted herself into a political force or expression. It would distort her perspective and make false her word. She must be herself, just as in any situation, agreeable or disagreeable, an honest person must first of all appear as he or she is, without dissembling.

The sincerity of the gospel is what is beautiful about the church. In times of calm or times of persecution, in ambiguities, in adversities, she is herself. The principal concern that I urge as pastor is that we build the kingdom of God, which the church has the great task of consolidating by being herself, without trying to fight with anyone or flatter anyone. Those who defend God's reign on earth as she does will get along with her, and those who oppose God's reign on earth will conflict with her.

OCTOBER 28, 1979

Let us not tire of denouncing the idolatry of wealth,
    which makes human greatness consist in having
and forgets that true greatness is in being.

One's value is not in what one has,
    but in what one is.

NOVEMBER 4, 1979

If we had time, we might examine at this point the message of
Puebla calling for the building of a civilization of love. But I just
want to say one thing. Many think that this call for love is inef-
fectual, is inadequate, is weak. This notion is so fixed that some
of the journalists who interview me often ask me, "Do you, who
preach love, believe that love can settle this? Don't you think
that violence is the only way if in the course of history only violence has achieved changes?"

I tell them, "If in fact that is how it has been, it is also a fact
that humans have not yet used the power that is distinctively
theirs. Humans are not characterized by brute force, they are
not mere animals. Humans are characterized by reason and by
love."

NOVEMBER 4, 1979

I want to assure you —
and I ask your prayers to be faithful to this promise —
that I will not abandon my people,
but together with them I will run all the risks
that my ministry demands.

NOVEMBER 11, 1979

In the measure in which we are church,
    that is, true Christians,
    incarnating the gospel,
in that measure we will be the timely citizens,
the Salvadorans needed at this moment.
If we retreat from this inspiration of God's word,
    we can be pragmatists,
    political opportunists,
but we will not be the sort of Christians
who are ever shapers of history.

NOVEMBER 11, 1979

With this people
it is not hard to be a good shepherd.
They are a people that impel to their service
us who have been called to defend their rights
    and to be their voice.

NOVEMBER 18, 1979

God and human beings make history.
God saves humanity in the history of one's own people.
The history of salvation will be El Salvador's history
when we Salvadorans seek in our history
the presence of God the Savior.

NOVEMBER 18, 1979

A Christian must be concerned to form community and to
see that the community keeps growing in depth of faith and
missionary extension. Christians must be dissatisfied as long as

they see so many baptized persons who have not perceived the richness of their baptism. What the apostles used to do was to take that treasure and make it greater by forming communities and community life.

This community sense is something we urgently need today in our country. At times there is confusion between the Christian community and the political group. Some are unable to tell the difference because the members of a community don't deepen their faith, and they get mixed up.

In my pastoral letter, I say that often our people, especially the young people, have reached political maturity earlier than Christian maturity; they see life more in political terms (as though the political dimension of life were the only one), and they have no time left for what is Christian. But it should be the other way around: what is Christian comes first, and it is thence that each one should discover his or her proper place in the country, in whatever vocation God gives one.

If God gives a political vocation, one should live it, but live it as a Christian. That way we'll have the sort of people needed nowadays, people who will become mature in a Christian community, who will mature in the gospel, in their faith, in their commitment to Christ, in their following of the Lord; people who will not let them betray him in the laws or customs of the land, that is, in political life. And they will then become the leaders of the transformations that the nation needs today more than ever, Christians thoroughly committed to Christ, in a community that is God's people and, as the Bible says, is like a light on a mountaintop.

Today, with so much confusion, so many groups, so many claims, the Christian community should consider itself a bright light, providing light and orientation to everything that happens around us.[130]

NOVEMBER 23, 1979

I'm deeply impressed by that moment when Christ
   stands alone before the world figured in Pilate.
The truth is left alone;
   his own followers have been afraid.
Truth is fearfully daring,
   and only heroes can follow the truth.
So much so that Peter,
   who has said he will die if need be,
flees like a coward,
   and Christ stands alone.

Let's not be afraid to be left alone
   if it's for the sake of the truth.
Let's be afraid to be demagogs,
   coveting the people's sham flattery.
If we don't tell them the truth,
   we commit the worst sin:
betraying the truth
   and betraying the people.

Christ would rather be left alone,
   but able to say before the world figured in Pilate:
Everyone who hears my voice
     belongs to the truth.[131]

NOVEMBER 25, 1979 (FEAST OF CHRIST THE KING)

"He loved us."[132] This is the first cause. God loved us, and his
love took concrete human form in Christ our Lord.

Christ standing before the sick, before the blind, before the
crippled, before the sinner — that is God's mercy, his love walking on this earth.

Who does not approach with tenderness the Lord's love
found in Christ Jesus? He lives on earth and loves us. And by

that love, says the book of Revelation, "he has freed us from our sins by his blood."

He knew that the Father was asking him for his own blood as the price of forgiveness, and he did not shrink from the awful sufferings of Good Friday. He surrendered himself.

His flesh held all our iniquities, says the prophet.[133] And God charged him the price of our liberation. No liberation is more profound than Christ's.

How ridiculous are liberations that talk only about having higher wages, about having more money and better prices! Liberations that talk only about political change, about who is in the government, are only bits and pieces of the great liberation, the one that paid for the root of all our ills, of all our injustices.

And if the earth's liberations don't mesh with this great liberation of Christ, the grand Liberator, then they are mutilated, not genuine liberations, only parts of liberation.

NOVEMBER 25, 1979

Historical moments will change,
　but God's design will ever be the same:
to save human beings in history.
Therefore, the church,
entrusted with carrying out God's design,
cannot be identified with any historical design.
The church could not be the ally of the Roman Empire
　or of Herod
　or of any king on earth
　or of any political system
　or of any human political strategy.
It will enlighten them all
but it will always remain authentically
　the one that proclaims salvation history,
　God's design.

DECEMBER 9, 1979

Let's not forget, dear Christians,
    that the church was born of sinners.
The church is holy, because it has God's Spirit
    giving it life;
but it is sinful and it needs conversion,
    because we make it up – humans tending toward evil
and at times perhaps with a past that shames us.

But once we are converted,
    we try –
we try! –
    to follow the Lord.
We don't follow him as yet with perfection,
but the effort to follow him
is what makes a true disciple of our Lord Jesus Christ.

DECEMBER 16, 1979

There aren't two categories of people.

There aren't some that were born to have everything,
    leaving the rest with nothing,
and a majority that has nothing
    and cannot taste the happiness
that God has created for all.

The Christian society that God wants
is one in which we share the goodness
that God has given for everyone.

DECEMBER 16, 1979

Conversion will be lasting and profound if we are able to criticize our false way of looking at the world and at people.

    I want to insist on this, because I think that what a mature Salvadoran most needs today is a critical sense.

Don't be waiting for which way the bishop will lean, or for what others will say, or what the organization says. Each one should be a critical man or woman.

By its fruits you will know the tree. Look at what it produces and criticize it according to what it does, whether it's the government, the people's political organization, the political party, or whatever group. Don't let yourselves be carried along and manipulated. It's you, the people, who must pass sentence in regard to what the people need.

You each have to see the world with your own eyes. You have to ignore your surroundings. I think: how many poor housemaids have to think the same as the lady of the house! It doesn't have to be that way; they should think freely. That's the way the masses are manipulated; many people are controlled through hunger.

You have to be critical and see the world and individuals using your own judgment, and Christians must learn to sharpen their distinctive Christian judgment.

The rich must be critical amid their own surroundings of affluence: why they are wealthy and why next door there are so many poor. A wealthy Christian will find there the beginning of conversion, in a personal questioning: why am I rich and all around me so many that hunger?

DECEMBER 16, 1979

Dear brothers and sisters who are economically powerful,
it is probable that at this moment,
faced with the threat of land reform,
you feel discouragement, fear, and perhaps hatred,
and have even decided to oppose by every means possible
    the reform's being carried out.
Probably there are some
who even would rather destroy everything

and radically harm the country's economy
than share with those
whose labor you have used for many years.
The church that has served you so much says to you today:
This is the moment to show yourselves generous Christians
and to love as Jesus has loved us,
who, being rich, made himself poor for our sake.

DECEMBER 16, 1979

The salvation that we preach in Christ's church is the same salvation that Mary believed in and that she initiated when she
gave her consent and became fruitful with God's salvation.

The church is zealous to guard Mary's belief, God's plan for
human salvation, and it will not let his plan be lost in merely
human plans. Rather, it must sanctify and permeate these. Every
people's liberation effort will be effective and according to
God's heart only if it lets faith in God's plan to save humanity
pervade it.

DECEMBER 23, 1979

We must not seek the child Jesus
in the pretty figures of our Christmas cribs.
We must seek him among the undernourished children
who have gone to bed tonight with nothing to eat,
among the poor newsboys
who will sleep covered with newspapers in doorways.

DECEMBER 24, 1979

The great mystery that Paul proclaims is what he states with total clarity in the epistle we have read today: "I was given to
know by revelation the mystery that had not been made known

to people in other times, which has been revealed now by the Spirit to his holy apostles and prophets" – to those charged with preaching.

What is the mystery? "That the gentiles too are coheirs, members of the same body, partakers of the promise in Christ Jesus through the gospel."[134] This is the great news!

Brothers and sisters who fill this cathedral, we are gentiles. We do not belong to the Jewish people; we are descendants of pagans who populated these lands just five centuries ago – primitive peoples, but God was thinking of us.

Who could have told Christopher Columbus that on these virgin lands, filled with forests and animals and Indians, would appear our cathedrals, our shrines, our churches, a Christian civilization? What a great mystery! You too, Indians of America, are called to partake of the heritage of Christ; you too, blacks of Africa, and you too, people of Asia and all the world, you are called.

JANUARY 6, 1980

To the oligarchy, I repeat what I said before: do not look on me as a judge or an enemy. I'm only the shepherd, the brother, the friend of this people, the one who knows of their suffering, of their hunger, of their affliction.

In the name of their voices, I raise my own to say: do not make idols of your riches; do not preserve them in a way that lets others die of hunger. One must share in order to be happy.

JANUARY 6, 1980

Christians who live out their baptism become saints and heroes. No one is worth more among the citizens of a country than baptized citizens who are faithful to their baptism. These are the sort of Christians of El Salvador that we want.

That is why we preach this way. We wish to shake our baptized people out of habits that threaten to make them practically baptized pagans, idolaters of their money and power. What sort of baptized persons are these? Those who want to bear the mark of the Spirit and the fire that Christ baptizes with must take the risk of renouncing everything and seeking only God's reign and his justice.

Salvadorans marked by Christ's baptism, which is Spirit and fire, must be Salvadorans of eternal hope; they cannot yield to pessimism. Neither must they let an earthly political program exhaust their ideals of eternal glory and triumph.

The great hope of baptized Salvadorans must stand above all the desperate plans of the earth's political leaders.

JANUARY 13, 1980

What an honor
    to think that all of you before me are Christ!
Even the humblest peasant,
    who may be pondering there next to a radio,
you are Christ!
For your baptism is one
with the death and resurrection
of the Lord.

JANUARY 13, 1980

In the most sublime homily ever given, Christ closes the book and says, "These things have been fulfilled today."[135]

That is what a homily is: saying that God's word is not a reading about times past, but a living and spiritual word that today is being fulfilled here. Hence our effort to apply God's eternal message to the people's concrete circumstances.

JANUARY 27, 1980

The homily is a sacred and liturgical discourse that carries the heart of the person hearing it to faith in God, praise of God, and celebration of the redemption that is made present in the eucharistic sacrifice.

We preach and we celebrate. Thus, the Mass is not complete if we only come to hear and do not stay for the eucharistic part. The main thing is not the preaching; that is only the path. The main thing is the moment when we adore Christ and give him our faith after being enlightened by the word. From there we go out into the world and make the word reality.

We hear the word, fit it to our circumstances, celebrate, are nourished in the life of Christ, and are led to commitment to duty, to home, and to service in the world for living a life that is truly according to God.

JANUARY 27, 1980

To know Christ is to know God.
Christ is the homily
that keeps explaining to us continually
    that God is love,
    that God is power,
    that the Spirit of the Lord is upon Jesus Christ,
    that he is the divine Word,
God's presence among us.

Jesus Christ and the gospel are not two separate things.
The gospel is not a biography of Christ;
for St. Paul, the gospel is the living power of God.
Reading the gospel is not like reading an ordinary book.
You have to fill yourself with faith
and stress the living Jesus Christ,
    the revelation of the Father.

You must feel, though it be in silence,
    without anyone's speaking,
    with deep faith in your heart,
that Christ is God's homily preaching to you
while you try to fill yourself with the divine power
that has come in Christ Jesus.

JANUARY 27, 1980

CHAPTER NINE

Good News to the Poor

"He has anointed me
  and sent me to give the good news to the poor."[136]

This is Christ's mission, to take the good news
  to the poor,
  to those who receive only bad news,
  to those who are always trampled by the powerful,
  to those who watch pass by, out of their reach,
    the riches that satisfy others.
The Lord comes for them,
  to make them happy
  and to tell them:
Do not covet.
Count yourselves happy and wealthy
  with the great gift brought to you
  by the one who being rich became poor
  to be with you.

JANUARY 27, 1980

I do not tire of telling everyone, especially young people who
long for their people's liberation, that I admire their social and
political sensitivity, but it saddens me when they waste it by going on ways that are false.

The church is telling them: this is the way, Christ's way. Put all your determination, all your self-giving, all your self-sacrifice, even to giving your lives, for the cause of the true liberation guaranteed by the one on whom God's Spirit is poured out. He will not show us false ways, and he will make his own the people's desire for liberation and justice. Their desire cries out to God, and God must hear that cry.

Let us, too, all take notice that the great leader of our liberation is the Lord's Anointed One, who comes to announce good news to the poor, to give freedom to the captives, to give news of the missing, to give joy to so many homes in mourning, so that society may be renewed as in the sabbatical years of Israel.

JANUARY 27, 1980

How beautiful will be the day when a new society,
instead of selfishly hoarding and keeping,
apportions, shares, divides up, and all rejoice
because we all feel we are children of the same God!
What else does God's word want in El Salvador's circumstances
but the conversion of all,
so that we can feel we are brothers and sisters?

JANUARY 27, 1980

I repeat what I told you once before when we feared
we might be left without a radio station:
God's best microphone is Christ,
and Christ's best microphone is the church,
and the church is all of you.
Let each one of you, in your own job, in your own vocation –
    nun, married person, bishop, priest,
    high school or university student,
    day laborer, wage earner, market woman –

each one in your own place live the faith intensely
and feel that in your surroundings
you are a true microphone of God our Lord.

JANUARY 27, 1980

God's program does not contradict the earth's programs.
It does contradict the sins of the earth's programs.
That is why the church has to proclaim God's reign –
   to remove sin from the earth's programs
   and to encourage the formation of programs
     in accord with God's reign.
This is the great work of Christians in history.

FEBRUARY 10, 1980

We are not political persons;
   we do not put our trust in merely human powers.
We are, above all, Christians, and we know
   that if the Lord does not build our civilization
all labor in vain who build it.

We know that our power comes from prayer
   and from our turning toward God.[137]

FEBRUARY 17, 1980

People do not mortify themselves during Lent
   out of a sick desire to suffer.
God did not make us for suffering.
If we fast or do penances or pray,
   it is for a very positive goal:
by overcoming self
   one achieves the Easter resurrection.
We do not just celebrate a risen Christ,

distinct from us,
but during Lent we prepare ourselves
    to rise with him to a new life
and to become the new persons
    that are what the country needs right now.
Let us not just shout slogans
    about new structures;
new structures will be worthless
    without new persons
to administer the new structures the country needs
    and live them out in their lives.

FEBRUARY 17, 1980

The Puebla document contains a statement that, rightly understood, fills us with hope:

Poverty is a palpable reality in Latin America – the stamp that marks the great mass of people. At the same time, these masses are not only open to receive the Beatitudes and the Father's predilection, but are capable of being the genuine protagonists of their own development.[138]

The poor are a sign in Latin America. The masses of our nations are poor, and for this reason they are capable of receiving God's gifts. And, when filled with God, they are able to transform their own societies.

FEBRUARY 17, 1980

The existence of poverty as a lack of what is necessary
    is an indictment.
Those who say the bishop, the church, and the priests
    have caused the bad state of the country
want to paper over the reality.
Those who have created the evil

are those who have made possible
the hideous social injustice our people live in.

Thus, the poor have shown the church the true way to go.
A church that does not join the poor,
   in order to speak out from the side of the poor
against the injustices committed against them,
is not the true church of Jesus Christ.

FEBRUARY 17, 1980

I told them at Louvain:[139]
Our world in El Salvador is not an abstraction.
It is not an example of what is meant by "the world"
   in developed countries like yours.
It is a world made up in the vast majority
   of poor and oppressed men and women.
That world of the poor, we say, is the key to understand
   the Christian faith, the church's activity,
and the political dimension
   of the faith and the church's activity.
The poor are the ones who tell us what the world is
   and what service the church must offer to the world.

FEBRUARY 17, 1980

Allow me, I said at Louvain, to speak for my people's poor, as
their representative, and explain briefly the circumstances and
the activity of our church in the world where we live. I went on
to tell them of what is happening to our church here in El Salvador and what we are doing.

    First, we become incarnate among the poor. We want a
church that is really side by side with the poor, with the people
of El Salvador. And as we draw near to the poor, we find we are

gradually uncovering the genuine face of the Suffering Servant of Yahweh. We are getting to know closer at hand the mystery of the Christ who becomes human and becomes poor for us.

What else does the church do here? It proclaims the good news to the poor, I said.

I do not mean this in the demagogic sense of shutting the door on others. On the contrary.

I do mean that those who have for centuries listened to bad news and lived even worse realities are now hearing from the church the word of Jesus: "The reign of God is near; it is yours! Blessed are you poor, for the reign of God is yours."[140]

Hence the church has good news to proclaim to the rich as well; they are to turn to the poor and thus share with them in the riches of God's reign that belong to the poor.

Another thing that the church does in El Salvador, I said, is its commitment to defend the poor. The poor masses of our land find in the church the voice of Israel's prophets. There are among us those who sell the just for money and the poor for a pair of sandals, as the prophets said. There are those who pile up spoils and plunder in their palaces, who crush the poor, who bring on a reign of violence while reclining on beds of ivory, who join house to house and field to field so as to take up all there is and remain alone in the land.[141]

These texts of the prophets are not distant voices that we read with reverence in our liturgy. They are daily realities, whose cruelty and vehemence we live each day.

And therefore, I told them, the church suffers the fate of the poor, which is persecution. Our church glories that it has mingled the blood of its priests, its catechists, and its communities with that of the massacred people and has continually borne the mark of persecution. Because it disquiets, it is slandered, and its voice crying against injustice is disregarded.

FEBRUARY 17, 1980

The church's good name is not a matter
   of being on good terms with the powerful.
The church's good name is a matter of knowing
   that the poor regard the church as their own,
of knowing that the church's life on earth
   is to call on all, on the rich as well,
to be converted and to be saved alongside the poor,
for they are the only ones called blessed.

FEBRUARY 17, 1980

Poverty is a force for liberation because, in addition to being an accusation of sin and a force of Christian spirituality, it is a commitment.

Christians, this word is for me first of all. I must give an example of being a Christian. And it is for all of you, my brother priests, and for you, religious, and for all baptized people who call yourselves Christians. Listen to what the Medellín conference says:

> Poverty, as a commitment that takes on voluntarily and out of love the condition of the needy of this world, in order to witness to the evil their condition represents and to spiritual freedom from wealth, follows in this the example of Christ, who made his own all the consequences of the sinful condition of humans and, "being rich, became poor" in order to save us.[142]

This is the commitment of being a Christian: to follow Christ in his incarnation. If Christ, the God of majesty, became a lowly human and lived with the poor and even died on a cross like a slave, our Christian faith should also be lived in the same way. The Christian who does not want to live this commitment of solidarity with the poor is not worthy to be called Christian.

Christ invites us not to fear persecution.
Believe me, brothers and sisters,

anyone committed to the poor
   must suffer the same fate as the poor.
And in El Salvador we know the fate of the poor:
   to be taken away,
   to be tortured,
   to be jailed,
   to be found dead.

Let whoever desires this world's privileges and not the persecutions that come from this commitment listen to the awesome
paradox in today's gospel: "Blessed are you when people hate
you and reject you and insult you and say you are evil, because
of the Son of Man. Rejoice on that day and leap for joy, because
your reward will be great in heaven."[143]

With great joy and gratitude I wish to congratulate our
priests. It is just when they are most committed to the poor
that they are most defamed. It is just when they are most at
the side of our people in their wretchedness that they are most
slandered.

I wish to rejoice with the religious men and women who have
taken their stand with our people, even to the point of hero-
ically suffering with them, and with the Christian communities
and with the catechists who stay at their posts while cowards
flee.

Let those who would flee the effects of persecution, of slander, of degradation, listen to what Christ says this Sunday:
"Woe to you when everyone speaks well of you! That is what
your ancestors did with the false prophets."[144]

FEBRUARY 17, 1980

We are especially sorry today, when we most need it, to be
without our radio station, YSAX, the instrument that carried
God's word forth from our Sunday Mass. As you all know, last

Monday the transmitter was destroyed by a bomb set by an ultrarightist group.

This new attack is a serious violation of freedom of expression. This attack is an attempt to silence the prophetic and pastoral voice of the archdiocese, simply because it is trying to be the voice of the voiceless, because it has reported the systematic violation of human rights, because it has tried to tell the truth, defend justice, and spread the Christian message.

From the times of Jesus, that message has shocked the powerful. It shocked the powerful of his time but, as now, was listened to and accepted by the poor and simple.

FEBRUARY 24, 1980

Moses commanded the citizens of Israel to take to the temple the first fruits of the harvest of their fields and to offer them to God with the following prayer, which contains Israel's creed:

> Then in the presence of the Lord your God you will say: "My father was a wandering Aramean who went down to Egypt and settled there with a few persons. Then they grew into a great, strong, and numerous race. The Egyptians mistreated and oppressed us, and imposed a harsh slavery on us. Then we cried out to the Lord, the God of our ancestors. The Lord heard our voice and looked on our oppression." [145]

And it goes on to describe how he took them out of Egypt and through the desert to give them their own country, a promised land.

Israel's creed is pure history. It begins with the promise to the patriarchs – unbelievable promises. An old man is promised he will be father of a numerous people, although he is childless and sterile. A people that has increased under slavery is told by God that he will give it a land where milk and honey flow. And this people sets out for the promised land, and when the promise becomes a reality, the fruits of that land are offered as the sign that God has kept his promise. The offering is Israel's Mass, like our own offering, where we give thanks for our land, for our country, recalling that God does not abandon the people.

It is a beautiful creed. The Israelites did not have an ethereal faith, like many Christians who think that speaking of things like this gets the church involved in politics. Israel's faith was the faith of its political life. Faith and political life were turned into a single act of love for the Lord. Their political life breathed God's graces and promises.

And the God of all peoples, the God of El Salvador as well, must be such a God, one that illumines political life also. He is the one who gives us our farmlands, and he is the one who wants land reform. He is the one who wants a more just distribution of the wealth that El Salvador produces. It is not right that some fill up their coffers and the people are left without the gifts of God that he has given for the people.

Israel's creed was inspired by the Holy Spirit, who gives unity to all of Israel's history. The Bible, which is the history of Israel's people, is like the Holy Spirit's own book. Although it was written by persons of different centuries and cultures, the Holy Spirit is the author of those pages of Israel's history that make up the Bible, a model for the histories of all peoples.

All of our peoples should read the Bible and learn from it the relationship of faith and politics. The Bible is the text from which to learn how to live that wonderful relationship between faith and political life. When the Holy Spirit brings Israel's times to their fullness and Christ is born through the Holy Spirit, this Christ begins to form a new people. We Christians are that people, and we as a people that arises are the work of the Holy Spirit.

God works out the history of salvation in each people's history. Each people is different from every other, and no imperial power may interfere to influence our people's way of being. The God of the great empires is the God who demands justice of the powerful in them and defends the poor of their people. He has plenty to do there. And the God of our impoverished peoples is also constructing the history of salvation, with El Salvador's history and not with artificial histories. History made alive by the Holy Spirit provides, in the resurrection, a wonderful incentive for the Christian people. The Spirit who raised up Christ has provided in the risen Christ a model for history. Towards the resurrection all histories must march. They must provide persons who will rise to freedom after living the way of the cross – indeed, to a freedom to be enjoyed on this earth, but that will not be definitive until we enjoy it in the fullness of God's kingdom.

That does not mean that we are going to leave the people's liberation for the other side of death. The risen Christ belongs now to present history, and he is the source of human liberty and dignity.

That is why we prepare for Easter by observing Lent, so that from our Salvadoran condition, living our Salvadoran Lent, we Salvadorans may enjoy the new life of the risen Christ, striving for a more just and fraternal country. There we can live more intensely the life of God that Christ has brought us and that he gives us through his paschal mystery.

Lent and Easter are our own, and each people can say so. Christ is our own. Christ is a Salvadoran for Salvadorans. Christ has risen here in El Salvador for us, so that with the power of the Spirit we can pursue our own nature, our own history, our own freedom, our own dignity as the Salvadoran people.

FEBRUARY 24, 1980

It does not matter to us what group wants to claim for itself the attack on our radio station. What matters is that, in the last analysis, those responsible are members of the oligarchy, which at this moment is desperately and blindly trying to repress the people. The dynamiting of YSAX is only a symbol. It shows that the oligarchy, seeing the danger of losing the complete domination they have over investment and over agricultural exports, as well as their near-monopoly of land, are defending their selfish interests – not with arguments, not with popular support, but with the only thing they have. They use their money to buy weapons and pay mercenaries who massacre the people and strangle every lawful cry for justice and freedom.

That is the reason for all the bombs set off in their name, like the one in the Central American University. And that is why they have murdered so many peasants, students, teachers, laborers, and other members of organizations.

FEBRUARY 24, 1980

Yesterday, when a journalist asked me
   where I found inspiration for my work and my preaching,
I told him: "Your question is very timely, for just now
   I have come from my retreat.
If it were not for this prayer and reflection
with which I try to stay united with God,
I would be no more than what St. Paul says:
clanging metal."

MARCH 2, 1980

This Lent, which we observe amid blood and sorrow, ought to presage a transfiguration of our people, a resurrection of our nation. The church invites us to a modern form of penance, of fasting and prayer – perennial Christian practices, but adapted to the circumstances of each people.

Lenten fasting is not the same thing in those lands where people eat well as is a Lent among our third-world peoples, undernourished as they are, living in a perpetual Lent, always fasting. For those who eat well, Lent is a call to austerity, a call to give away in order to share with those in need. But in poor lands, in homes where there is hunger, Lent should be observed in order to give to the sacrifice that is everyday life the meaning of the cross.

But it should not be out of a mistaken sense of resignation. God does not want that. Rather, feeling in one's own flesh the consequences of sin and injustice, one is stimulated to work for social justice and a genuine love for the poor. Our Lent should awaken a sense of social justice.

Let us observe our Lent thus, giving our sufferings, our bloodshed, our sorrow the same value that Christ gave to his own condition of poverty, oppression, abandonment, and injustice. Let us change all that into the cross of salvation that redeems the world and our people. And with hatred for none, let us be converted and share both joys and material aids, in our poverty, with those who may be even needier.

MARCH 2, 1980

Let us see to it that Christ is in the midst of our people's political movement. Let us us not let Christ be absent from our history.

That is what is most important at this moment of our nation's history: that Christ be God's glory and power, and that the scandal of the cross and of pain not make us flee from Christ and cast aside suffering. Instead, let us embrace it.

MARCH 2, 1980

This is the hour of political programs for El Salvador. But they are political programs that are worthless unless they try to reflect God's program.

The pastor's mission, the church's mission, is not to enter into competition by proposing one more program. Rather, with the autonomy and freedom of God's children offered by the gospel, our mission is to indicate what may be good in each program in order to encourage it, and what may be bad in any program in order to remove it.

MARCH 2, 1980

There can be no true liberation
    until people are freed from sin.
All the liberationist groups that spring up in our land
    should bear this in mind.
The first liberation to be proposed by a political group
    that truly wants the people's liberation
must be to free oneself from sin.
While one is a slave of sin —
    of selfishness, violence, cruelty, and hatred —
one is not fitted for the people's liberation.

MARCH 2, 1980

The church in Latin America
    has much to say about humanity.
It looks at the sad picture
    portrayed by the Puebla conference:
faces of landless peasants
    mistreated and killed by the forces of power,
faces of laborers arbitrarily dismissed
    and without a living wage for their families,
faces of the elderly,

faces of outcasts,
faces of slum dwellers,
faces of poor children who from infancy
    begin to feel the cruel sting of social injustice.
For them, it seems, there is no future –
    no school, no high school, no university.
By what right have we cataloged persons
    as first-class persons or second-class persons?
In the theology of human nature there is only one class:
children of God.

MARCH 2, 1980

Let us not think that our dead
    have gone away from us.
Their heaven, their eternal reward,
    makes them perfect in love;
they keep on loving the same causes
    for which they died.
Thus, in El Salvador the force of liberation
    involves not only those who remain alive,
but also all those whom others have tried to kill
    and who are more present than before
in the people's movement.

MARCH 2, 1980

The great need today
    is for Christians who are active and critical,
who don't accept situations without analyzing them
    inwardly and deeply.
We no longer want masses of people
    like those who have been trifled with for so long.
We want persons like fruitful fig trees,

who can say yes to justice and no to injustice
and can make use of the precious gift of life,
    regardless of the circumstances.

MARCH 9, 1980

Nothing is so important to the church as human life,
as the human person,
above all, the person of the poor and the oppressed.
Besides being human beings,
they are also divine beings,
since Jesus said that whatever is done to them
he takes as done to him.
That bloodshed, those deaths,
are beyond all politics.
They touch the very heart of God.

MARCH 16, 1980

As pastor, I invite you to listen
    to the hoarse, imperfect echo of my words.
But do not regard the instrument; regard the one
    who bids me tell you of God's infinite love.
Be converted! Be reconciled!
    Love one another!
Fashion a people of the baptized,
    a family of God's children!
Those who think that my preaching is political,
    that it incites to violence,
as though I were the cause
    of all the evils in the land,
forget that the church's word
    does not invent the evils in the world;

it casts a light on them.
The light shows what is there,
  it does not create it.
The great evil is already there,
  and God's word wants to undo those evils.
It points them out, as it must,
  for people to return to right ways.

MARCH 16, 1980

At this time, when land in El Salvador is the object of conflict, let us not forget that the land is closely tied to God's blessings and promises.

Israel now had its own land. "I will give you all this land," God had told the patriarchs, and after the captivity, led forth by Moses and Joshua, here was the land. And so they celebrated a grand thanksgiving rite, Israel's first Passover.[146]

It is a call to us to celebrate, with equal gratitude, adoration, and acknowledgment, the God who saves us. God has brought us too out of bondage. The God we put our hope in for our liberations is the God of Israel, the God who today receives the celebration of the first Passover.

There is a theological meaning in the bond between reconciliation and the land. I want to emphasize this idea because it seems to me very appropriate. Not to have land is a consequence of sin. Adam leaves Paradise as a man without land. It is the effect of sin. Now, with God's forgiveness, Israel returned to the land. They ate ears of grain from their own land, the fruits of their land. God gave his blessing in the sign of the land.

The land contains much that is of God. That is why it groans when the unjust monopolize it and leave no land for others. Land reform is a theological necessity. A country's land cannot stay in a few hands. It must be given to all, and all must share in God's blessings on the land.

Each country has its own promised land in the territory that geography has allotted it. We must always bear in mind and never forget this theological reality: the land is a sign of justice and reconciliation. There will be no true reconciliation between our people and God as long as there is no just distribution, as long as the goods of the earth in El Salvador are not for the benefit and happiness of all Salvadorans.

MARCH 16, 1980

God in Christ dwells near at hand to us.
Christ has given us a guideline:
    "I was hungry and you gave me to eat."
Where someone is hungry, there is Christ near at hand.
    "I was thirsty and you gave me to drink."
When someone comes to your house to ask for water,
    it is Christ, if you look with faith.
In the sick person longing for a visit Christ tells you,
    "I was sick and you came to visit me."
        Or in prison.[147]
How many today are ashamed to testify for the innocent!
What terror has been sown among our people
    that friends betray friends whom they see in trouble!
If we could see that Christ is the needy one,
    the torture victim,
the prisoner,
    the murder victim,
and in each human figure
    so shamefully thrown by our roadsides
could see Christ himself cast aside,
we would pick him up like a medal of gold
    to be kissed lovingly.
We would never be ashamed of him.
How far people are today –

especially those who torture and kill
and value their investments more than human beings –
from realizing that all the earth's millions
    are good for nothing,
    are worthless, compared to a human being.
The person is Christ,
    and in the person viewed and treated with faith
we look on Christ the Lord.

MARCH 16, 1980

To try to reveal Christ
    is our great pastoral task.
If I speak of earthly matters or political questions,
    it is to guide our reflection towards Christ.
I would like you to understand me well
    so as not to have a wrong idea of these Masses.
Far from being political gatherings,
    they mean to draw the people toward Christ,
    toward God.
Thus they are understood in many testimonials I receive.
It gives me great comfort to know
    that people come to church on Sunday to look for Christ.
Even in the criminal realities of our land
Christ is present,
    rejecting all that crime.
That is why we must speak of it here.

MARCH 16, 1980

I feel more pity than anger
    when they insult me and slander me.
I feel pity for those poor blind people

who can't see beyond the person.
Let them know that I hold no animosity,
    no grudge.
Those anonymous letters that come
    don't offend me with all their raging,
nor what is said through other means
    or lived out in the heart.
It's not a pity of superiority,
    but a pity of thankfulness to God
and of prayer to God:
    Lord, open their eyes.
    Lord, let them be converted.
    Lord, instead of the bitterness of hate
        that they live in their hearts,
let them live the joy of reconciliation with you.

MARCH 16, 1980

This is the fundamental thought of my preaching:
Nothing is so important to me as human life.
Taking life is something so serious, so grave –
    more than the violation of any other human right –
because it is the life of God's children,
and because such bloodshed only negates love,
awakens new hatreds,
makes reconciliation and peace impossible.

MARCH 16, 1980

Easter is itself now the cry of victory.
No one can quench the life that Christ has resurrected.
Neither death nor all the banners of death and hatred

raised against him and against his church can prevail.
He is the victorious one!

Just as he will thrive in an unending Easter,
so we must accompany him in a Lent and a Holy Week
    of cross, sacrifice, and martyrdom.
As he said, blessed are they who are not scandalized
    by his cross.

Lent, thus, is a call to celebrate our redemption
    in that difficult combination of cross and victory.
Our people are well prepared to do so these days:
    all that surrounds us proclaims the cross.
But those who have Christian faith and hope
    know that behind this calvary of El Salvador
lies our Easter,
    our resurrection.
That is the Christian people's hope.

MARCH 23, 1980

I have no ambition for power,
and so with complete freedom
I tell the powerful
    what is good and what is bad,
and I tell any political group
    what is good and what is bad.
That is my duty.

MARCH 23, 1980

God's program to liberate the people is a transcendent one.
Transcendence gives liberation its true and definitive dimension. I suppose I repeat this idea too much, but I will keep on

saying it. In wanting to give immediate solutions to immediate problems, we run the great danger of forgetting that immediate solutions can be mere band-aids and not real solutions. A genuine solution must fit into God's ultimate program. Whatever solution we may decide on – for better land distribution, for a better management of money in El Salvador, for a political arrangement suited to the common good of Salvadorans – will have to be found always in the context of definitive liberation.

MARCH 23, 1980

"God's reign is already present on our earth in mystery.
When the Lord comes, it will be brought to perfection."[148]

That is the hope that inspires Christians.
We know that every effort to better society,
especially when injustice and sin are so ingrained,
is an effort that God blesses,
    that God wants,
    that God demands of us.[149]

MARCH 24, 1980

Notes

1 Oscar Romero became archbishop of San Salvador on February 22, 1977, after several priests had been expelled from the country and while the church of the archdiocese was under attack in the media. On March 12, Rutilio Grande, the pastor of the rural parish of Aguilares, was ambushed and murdered, along with two parishioners. This selection is from the funeral homily.

2 Matthew 25:40.

3 In mid-May, military forces raided the town of Aguilares, the parish of the murdered Father Rutilio Grande, killed dozens of people, desecrated the church and the eucharist, and deported the three remaining priests. The archbishop was not allowed to visit the parish, which remained occupied for days. By June 19, the parish buildings were once again in church hands, and Archbishop Romero was able to install a new parish team, consisting of a priest and three nuns. Thousands attended the installation Mass and heard the homily from which these selections are taken.

4 Luke 9:23.

5 Sirach 31:10.

6 Jeremiah 38:4.

7 Jeremiah 20:7–10.

8 Luke 1:49.

9 Exodus 3:7.

10 Luke 12:51.

11 Luke 21:18–19.

12 Luke 23:35–43.

13 Archbishop Romero preached at a Mass for the mothers and other family members of persons who had disappeared while in the custody of government security forces.

14 Romans 8:28.

15 Archbishop Romero preached this homily at a Mass at which he administered the sacrament of confirmation.

16 Matthew 28:20, 16:18.

17 Archbishop Romero preached this homily at the ordination of two priests.

18 December 12 is the feast of Our Lady of Guadalupe, patroness of Latin America. In 1531, an Indian, Juan Diego, reported that Mary had appeared to him, and he showed her image left on his cloak, which is now venerated in the Guadalupe basilica in Mexico City. Archbishop Romero preached this homily in the church of Our Lady of Guadalupe in San Salvador.

19 Death squads murdered Father Rutilio Grande, S.J., on March 12, 1977, and Father Alfonso Navarro on May 11, 1977.

20 Matthew 25:41; Luke 9:26.

21 Isaiah 9:1–2.

22 Readings for the feast of the Epiphany (or Manifestation) of Christ: Isaiah 60:1–6; Ephesians 3:2–3, 5–6; Matthew 2:1–12.

23 Luke 15:31.

24 Mark 2:27.

25 Pope Paul VI, "The Development of Peoples," 20.

26 See Matthew 4:12–17.

27 Matthew 4:15–16; Isaiah 9:1–2.

28 Zephaniah 2:3; 3:12–13.

29 Matthew 5:1–12.

30 Sunday readings: Isaiah 58:7–10; 1 Corinthians 2:1–5; Matthew 5:13–16.

31 1 Corinthians 2:3.

32 1 Corinthians 2:1–2.

33 John 4:23–24.

34 Matthew 16:24.

35 Acts 5:29.

36 This is a column that Archbishop Romero wrote for the arch-
diocesan newspaper. It alludes to some of the attacks made on
him and the archdiocese in the secular media, owned by members
of the Salvadoran oligarchy. Radio and newspaper commentators
and paid advertisements often attacked him, accusing him of de-
viating from Catholic teaching and even of supporting communism and terrorism, because of his support of the rights of the
poor.

37 Acts 2:23.

38 1 Peter 3:15.

39 Exodus 3:12.

40 John 3:18.

41 From a newspaper column.

42 Matthew 18:7.

43 Genesis 4:10–11.

44 1 Corinthians 10:14–21.

45 A newspaper column.

46 "The Church in the Modern World," 74.

47 "The Church in the Modern World," 74.

48 Sunday readings: Hosea 6:3–6; Romans 1:18–25;
Matthew 9:9–13.

49 Genesis 12:1.

50 Matthew 11:25–26.

51 Luke 4:18.

52 Matthew 13:1–23.

53 Romans 8:18.

54 Wisdom 12:13, 16–19.

55 Acts 5:29.

56 Matthew 13:24–43.

57 See Romans 8:26–27.

58 From a newspaper column.

59 El Salvador celebrates the Feast of the Transfiguration, August 6, as the feast of its patron, the Divine Savior of the World. Readings of the Mass: Daniel 7:9–10, 13–14; 2 Peter 1:16–19; Matthew 17:1–9.

60 "Divine Revelation," 3.

61 Matthew 23:8.

62 In 1968, an assembly of the Latin American bishops met in Medellín, Colombia, to consider how to apply the teachings of Vatican Council II (1962–1965) to Latin America. The conclusions of the Medellín conference marked a turning point in the history of the church in Latin America, calling attention to the massive poverty of the people and calling for profound and widespread social change.

63 Romans 12:1–2.

64 Matthew 18:15–20.

65 Ezekiel 33:9–10.

66 Matthew 18:20.

67 Romans 13:8–10.

68 Readings: Isaiah 55:6–9; Philippians 1:20–24, 27; Matthew 20:1–16.

69 See Philippians 1:13.

70 Philippians 4:8.

71 Isaiah 25:7–8.

72 A newspaper column.

73 "The Church in the Modern World," 19.

74 "The Church in the Modern World," 20.

75 "The Church in the Modern World," 19.

76 "The Church in the Modern World," 19.

77 Luke 4:18.

78 Luke 1:53.

79 Sunday readings: Isaiah 40:1–5, 9–11; 2 Peter 3:8–14;
    Mark 1:1–8.

80 From a newspaper column.

81 1 Thessalonians 5:16–17.

82 1 Thessalonians 5:24.

83 1 Thessalonians 5:19.

84 1 Thessalonians 5:21.

85 Matthew 8:5–13; Luke 7:2–10.

86 See Psalm 104:30.

87 See "The Church in the Modern World," 22.

88 Luke 2:11, 14.

89 Archbishop Romero is referring to the 1968 general conference
    of Latin American bishops at Medellín, Colombia, which said:
    "We know that many families in Latin America have been inca-
    pable of educating in the faith, either because they are unstable or
    have disintegrated, or because they have imparted this education
    in purely traditional terms, at times with mythical and supersti-
    tious aspects. From this situation springs the necessity of bestow-
    ing on today's families the elements which will rebuild their
    evangelizing capacity in accordance with the doctrine of the
    church" (*The Church in the Present-Day Transformation of Latin America in
    the Light of the Council*, Latin American Episcopal Council, Bogotá,
    Colombia, 1970, official English version, p. 88).

90 Luke 2:34.

91 The Latin American bishops' conference that met at Puebla,
    Mexico, in 1979, was a follow-up to the Medellín conference (see
    note numbers 62 and 89).

92 This is an excerpt from the homily delivered at the funeral Mass
    of Father Octavio Ortiz and four young men killed by security
    forces that raided a retreat house where a youth group was gath-
    ered for a retreat. A crowd of thousands gathered before the
    doors of the cathedral for the Mass on Sunday morning. "In the
    evening of life you will be judged on love" is a paraphrase of

words of St. John of the Cross, the fifteenth-century Spanish mystic and poet.

93 A nuncio is a Vatican ambassador.

94 Press conference, Puebla, Mexico. Archbishop Romero attended the Latin American bishops' conference at Puebla, January 27 to February 13, 1979.

95 This is taken from Archbishop Romero's first Sunday homily after returning from the Puebla conference, at which the Latin American bishops expressed the church's "option for the poor."

96 See Matthew 25:31–46.

97 Exodus 19:8; 24:3.

98 Exodus 20:13.

99 Matthew 5:21–22.

100 Readings: Jeremiah 31:31–34; Hebrews 5:7–9; John 12:20–33.

101 From a newspaper column.

102 John 13:35.

103 Readings: Acts 10:34, 37–43; Colossians 3:1–5; John 20:1–9.

104 Readings: Acts 4:32–35; 1 John 5:1–6; John 20:19–31.

105 Interview in *Vida Nueva*.

106 Mass for Father Rafael Palacios, assassinated on June 20. He was the fifth priest murdered while Oscar Romero was archbishop.

107 Matthew 25:40.

108 2 Corinthians 8:14.

109 Sunday readings: Ezekiel 2:2–5; 2 Corinthians 12:7–10; Mark 6:1–6.

110 A newspaper column.

111 "Evangelization in the Modern World," 48.

112 Sunday readings: Amos 7:12–15; Ephesians 1:3–14; Mark 6:7–13.

113 Genesis 1:28.

114 Sunday readings: Jeremiah 23:1–6; Ephesians 2:13–18; Mark 6:30–34.

115 See Galatians 5:13.

116 In his Sunday homilies, Archbishop Romero always included an account of events of the week gone by.

117 Matthew 11:25.

118 From a newspaper column.

119 Mark 7:7.

120 Matthew 21:13.

121 James 1:21.

122 See Deuteronomy 4:1. Applause interrupted Archbishop Romero at this point.

123 Matthew 25:40.

124 Sunday readings: Numbers 11:25–29; James 5:1–6; Mark 9:37–42, 46–47.

125 See Galatians 5:13.

126 Mark 10:28.

127 Medellín, "Pastoral Concern for the Elites," 20.

128 Puebla, 1247.

129 Puebla, 1249.

130 Address to catechists.

131 Readings: Daniel 7:13–14; Revelation 1:5–8; John 18:33–37.

132 Revelation 1:5.

133 Isaiah 53:4–6.

134 Ephesians 3:2–6.

135 Luke 4:21.

136 Luke 4:18.

137 Sunday readings: Jeremiah 17:5–8; 1 Corinthians 15:12, 16–20; Luke 6:17, 20–26.

138 Puebla, 1129.

139 On February 2, 1980, Archbishop Romero received an honorary degree from the University of Louvain, Belgium.

140 See Mark 1:15; Luke 6:20.

141 See Amos 6:3–4; Isaiah 5:8.

142 "Poverty of the Church," 4c; 2 Corinthians 8:9.

143 Luke 6:22–23.

144 Luke 6:26.

145 Deuteronomy 26:5–7.

146 Joshua 5:10–12.

147 Matthew 25:35–36.

148 Vatican Council II, "The Church in the Modern World," 39.

149 This final passage was spoken only minutes before Romero's sudden death; as he concluded a homily during a service in a San Salvador hospital, he was killed by an assassin who entered the chapel from the back door and shot him.

Also of Interest

Oscar Romero
Reflections on His Life and Writings
Marie Dennis, Renny Golden, Scott Wright
ISBN 1-57075-309-1

"It is an extraordinary privilege to read this account of
Oscar Romero because it reveals his deep inner spirit. To
know him in this way becomes a call to find the face of God
in the poor as he did and to live the way of gospel love,
whatever the cost."
–*Bishop Thomas J. Gumbleton*

Voice of the Voiceless
The Four Pastoral Letters and Other Statements
Archbishop Oscar Romero
Introduction by Jon Sobrino
0-88344-525-5

Witnesses to the Kingdom
The Martyrs of El Salvador and the Crucified Peoples
Jon Sobrino
ISBN 1-57075-468-3

These essays on the role and meaning of martyrdom contain
poignant personal memories of Archbishop Romero and of
his Jesuit brothers, and of their legacy for the church.

Please support your local bookstore, or call 1-800-258-5838.
For a free catalogue, please write us at

Orbis Books, Box 308

Maryknoll NY 10545-0308

or visit our website at www.orbisbooks.com

Thank you for reading *The Violence of Love*. We hope you enjoyed it.